WHEN
YESTERDAY
BECOMES
TOMORROW

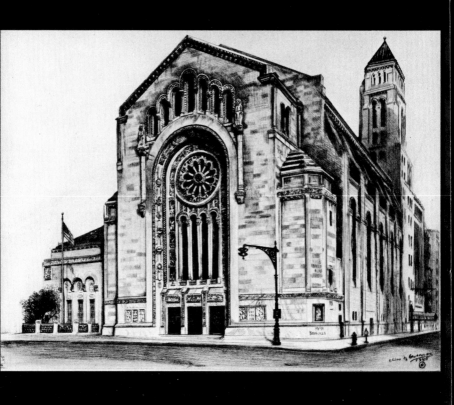

TEMPLE EMANU-EL
Fifth Avenue at Sixty-fifth Street
Dedicated 1930

WHEN YESTERDAY BECOMES TOMORROW

125th Anniversary Celebration

CONGREGATION EMANU-EL
OF THE CITY OF NEW YORK

1845 – 1970

Clearly then, the surface of events and the flow of words are not likely to be helpful for assessing long-run trends . . . What one must do is to view the present as though it were past, to view today as though it were already yesterday, and tomorrow as though it were today . . . We can make intelligible not only the seemingly confused and inchoate past but much of the bewildering and agonizing present as well. This will also reveal the grounds for my confidence that we are, despite signs to the contrary, on the threshold of the *Age of Humanity*.

I am confident that when yesterday becomes tomorrow, it will reveal that Temple Emanu-El was loyal to the principles on which it was founded: that at a time when the pangs of birth were mistaken for the agony of death, its rabbis and leaders discerned the distinction.

ELLIS RIVKIN

In an age of exceedingly rapid change, little thought and less time is given to a remembrance of things past. Our young people tell us that they are not as greatly concerned with yesterday's dreams and promises as they are with the inexorable demands of today and the urgent needs of tomorrow. "Now" is the important word in youth's lexicon, and older people for many reasons, not all good, are using the language of the young.

Thus it was that we determined to make one of the lesser "big celebrations" important. People who don't regard other big occasions as significant still are reverential of a centennial. The next important one is five hundred and then a thousand. One hundred and twenty-five is nothing special to shout about unless you are determined to make it so.

Borrowing slightly from the young, we ignored or outdebated the elders who said, "No one will be interested in a high-level lecture series." We had such a series and people did come in considerable numbers and were delighted and stimulated by what they saw, heard, and learned.

This book is a memento of our celebration. The lectures contained herein were greatly appreciated by those who heard them. It is our hope that they will gratify those who read them. All of us at Emanu-El are grateful to Mr. Alvin E. Coleman, President of the Congregation, for his encouragement throughout the months of our 125th anniversary celebration; to the Board of Trustees for its generous support of our efforts; and very particularly to Mr. Herbert C. Bernard, Chairman of the Anniversary Committee, who was indefatigable in his supervision of every aspect of the celebration. My associates, Rabbi Ronald B. Sobel and Rabbi Mark N. Goldman, were always near at hand with good counsel and encouragement. Mr. Henry Fruhauf, as ever, was helpful in making easier everybody's assignment. His part in the preparation of this Memorial Volume is especially appreciated.

Nathan A. Perilman
Senior Rabbi, Congregation Emanu-El

April 11, 1970
5th of Nisan, 5730

Fellow Members of Congregation Emanu-El and Friends:

It is a great pleasure and privilege for me to be able to welcome you here today to celebrate this significant anniversary of our eminent congregation. I must confess to feeling quite humble to be standing here in this holy pulpit, from which so many men of true distinction have addressed this congregation.

We should be mindful of the fact that all these happy events—our having become such an important congregation, our happy history for 125 years, and our freedom to celebrate today as we are doing—are inseparable parts of the priceless heritage of being a part of this most humane and superlative land, wherein we are all blessed to be citizens.

In itself, this celebration is unique, not so much because no other cultural institution has celebrated a 125th anniversary, or even that no other synagogue has so celebrated, but because this anniversary happens to fall at this particular time, when so many old values are being questioned and so many new "rights" are being asserted—among these, the "right" to deny "rights" to others.

I am certain that one of our most cherished freedoms and one of our greatest rights is the privilege to celebrate as we do today. We have worshiped as we chose for 125 years, in this very great country of ours. We pray that the time will never come when this freedom will be denied to anyone or when anyone will worship in fear. The values that our fathers, the founders of this great congregation, held in high esteem included respect for religion and its teachers—a need for worship and for showing reverence to deity. It is obvious that such values are not so highly esteemed today, and because they are not, we are in confusion and turmoil.

I hope that our participation in this unique event will bring us joy and renewed strength and will enable us once more to reassess our values as of old. Let us take great joy in our anniversary and look forward with hope to continued celebrations of similar anniversaries by our descendants, under like conditions of pride and freedom, for generations to come.

Alvin E. Coleman
President, Congregation Emanu-El

125th Anniversary Service
April 11, 1970

Contents

WHEN
YESTERDAY
BECOMES
TOMORROW

Will Science Destroy Society?*

EARL UBELL
Science Editor, WCBS-TV News

When Temple Emanu-El was founded 125 years ago, rationality was enough; intellectuals felt that rationality could
solve the world's problems, if only we could think hard
enough and marshal the forces of intellect in the service of
man. Today, rationality is not enough. Along with thought,
we need the services of science and technology. For a clue
to the nature of science, let me quote Lord Kelvin at the
turn of the century:

When you can measure what you are speaking about and

*This lecture was delivered spontaneously from notes and then edited by
me. However, I have tried to retain the informal flavor of the talk and
therefore have avoided "tightening" the arguments or adding too much
confirmatory detail.

3

express it in numbers, you know something about it; but when you cannot measure it, when you cannot express it in numbers, your knowledge is of a meager and unsatisfactory kind; it may be the beginning of knowledge, but you have scarcely, in your thoughts, advanced to the stage of science.

To many, Lord Kelvin seems old-fashioned, because there are many who parade a still older scholasticism under the banner of science. But there is no number in it; a lot of beautiful writing, perhaps, a lot of idiosyncratic observation, but not science. Nor do people differentiate between science and technology. Once there was a great gap between them: science was a gentleman's game played in the interest of finding out why; technology was a craftsman's game devoted to making things better. The distinction holds somewhat today, but the two are so interdigitated that one can hardly separate them. Progress in science depends inexorably on progress in technology and vice versa.

Today a lot of people are frightened by science and technology. They look around them and they see our air being polluted by products of technology, by automobiles, by smokestacks, by manufacturing processes. They see our water supplies threatened, our forests being annihilated, and because of our highways and rapid urbanization, our pristine land disappearing. Actually, at present, the land in the United States produces less oxygen (via green plants) than we now consume. We import our oxygen from the Pacific Ocean.

As for science, they see it as the mother of technology; in particular, of a lethal technology. Dr. Thomas Gold, professor of astronomy at Cornell, a very bright and imaginative

4

man, has a story that illustrates the connection. The story is in response to a question: "Why is it that we on earth have never been visited by beings from other planets in our universe?"

I know that some of you believe that we have been and are being visited by such beings, but the evidence is so strongly against it, I take non-visit as fact. But we may not be alone in this vast universe of ours with its trillions upon trillions of galaxies, each with billions of stars. Among those trillions of stars, there must be billions of stars like our own sun with systems of planets containing planets like our own little earth in this corner of our Milky Way galaxy.

Therefore, one would expect that there must be in our universe billions upon billions of planets which have life on them. For many of them—who can say precisely?—evolution of humanoid life must have progressed far beyond life as it exists on earth in 1969—perhaps 10,000 years beyond. And therefore, with these additional 10,000 years of technology, they could have developed techniques for traveling across interstellar and intergalactic space and visited us here.

One answer may be that they know that the earth may be a nice place to visit but not to live on.

A greater deterrent is distance. The distance between us and the nearest possible life-supporting planet is so enormous that to travel across it one needs not a little spaceship like a Mercury or Gemini, or even one so spacious as Apollo, but something the size of a small planet peopled by generations of those humanoids, traveling across interstellar voids, living, dying, and being sustained by a source of energy aboard that little planet. The energy is needed not only to keep the population alive but to drive the ship across billions upon billions of miles at very high speeds. What is that energy source? Atomic energy; in particular, hydrogen fusion energy.

If you fuse, i.e., melt together, two hydrogen atoms, you can release an enormous amount of energy. Science discovered the principle almost forty years ago, and technology achieved it in practice less than twenty years ago. The trouble is that the only way we can release the energy of hydrogen fusion is in one big bang of the hydrogen bomb. Although the suggestion has been made that hydrogen bombs exploded behind spaceships be used to drive them through space, I'm afraid the technique would shake up the passengers a bit. Besides, it's inefficient.

A more interesting scheme would be to scoop up hydrogen atoms in space (there's one for each cubic centimeter of space) and then release the energy of fusion slowly and in a controlled way both to generate electricity to sustain the population and to squirt hydrogen atoms out the rear end of the space ship to propel it forward. Although our scientists have been working on the slow release of hydrogen energy for twenty-five years, they have not succeeded. They have the hydrogen bomb, but not the slow release of fusion energy.

So one would imagine that a civilization on some distant planet would have solved the problem and traveled across the heavens with it. Why haven't they done it? That's Dr. Gold's question. Maybe they have done it and visited some other planet and we don't know it. But there's another answer. It goes this way.

It is in the nature of things that any technical society would first discover how to make hydrogen bombs. Then it takes at least twenty-five years to make the second discovery, the slow release of hydrogen fusion. It may take fifty years. We haven't done it yet.

But having the hydrogen bomb, those other societies never survived long enough to make the second discovery.

That is a sad proposition, sad for us because it gives us a very pessimistic view of the situation we face in 1969. Having invented not only the hydrogen bomb but the uranium and plutonium bombs, we have before us the question: will we survive those inventions, inventions born from science and raised by technology?

Yet there are other things that we have invented in the twentieth century which threaten us. They threaten us through annihilation, exhaustion, and extinction. So, you see, being a science editor is not all fun. There are nights when I lie awake thinking about these things. One reason that I tell you about them is to have company on those nights: so I will know that somebody else is also lying awake, thinking about annihilation, exhaustion, and extinction.

First, annihilation. As I said, we have hydrogen bombs and we have in the United States some 2,000 intercontinental ballistic missiles on submarines scattered over the oceans and in silos in the northern part of the United States. Those missiles are targeted; you know the targets—Moscow, Leningrad, Peking, and up to the last French election, one almost believed that Paris was included.

And on the other side of the world, in the Soviet Union, there is another forest of missiles—750 of them, or 1,500, the exact number depends on how much the Department of Defense (the U.S. Department of Defense) wants to scare us during budget season. The targets are New York, Washington, Detroit, Los Angeles . . . Peking? These are two forests of missiles facing each other. This is the balance of terror of which J. Robert Oppenheimer spoke. Once unleashed, these two doomsday machines go into action and there is no retreat. In thirty minutes it would all be over.

It has been underestimated how dreadful a nuclear holocaust will be. The movie *On the Beach*, based on the novel by Nevil Shute, purports to depict the effects of a nuclear war. Produced by Stanley Kramer and starring Gregory Peck and Ava Gardner, the film tells the story of a nuclear war which broke out in the Northern Hemisphere and so contaminated the atmosphere with radioactivity that eventually the radioactive clouds moved into the Southern Hemisphere to kill everyone.

The scene is set in Australia, where the last group of human beings hold out against the clouds. Gregory Peck, an American submarine commander stranded in Australia during the hostilities, has survived long enough to fall in love with Ava Gardner. As the effect of the radioactivity increases and people get sick, they retreat to their apartments, take suicide pills, and die: very quietly. They make no noise, no fuss; they just go away and die. At the end, Gregory Peck climbs into his submarine to steam back toward the United States because his men want to die near their country, and Ava Gardner is on the beach waving goodbye. I think teenagers today might call that a fun-death.

Alas! Nuclear war is grimmer than that. The British film

War Games depicts the immediate horror of a nuclear blast: the blinded babies; the flayed bodies; the fires. Even more of a horror is the social disaster. If we know anything, the bonds of society that keep us civilized break when a population is denuded of its people. The black plagues of the twelfth and thirteenth centuries, which killed, it is estimated, a third of Europe, pushed civilization to the brink, and were it not for the Catholic Church, the entire European continent might have been reduced to marauding bands of Neanderthals.

If you want to get a very good picture of what happens when a society is isolated from law and order—to use a terrible phrase—I suggest you read *The Painted Bird* by Jerzy Kosinski. It is the story of a little village in Poland during World War II into which a Polish child stumbles who looks Jewish but isn't. The people, lacking any social order, succumb to greed, cruelty, depravity, murder. I think we face that under nuclear threat.

Moreover, we face a nuclear holocaust that can essentially eliminate American, British, and European societies as we recognize them. Up until very recently, the Chinese did not see nuclear war as a threat. They called nuclear weapons paper tigers because they felt that in a nuclear war 200 million Americans would die, 200 million Europeans would die, 200 million Russians, and 200 million Chinese, leaving 500 million Chinese to take over the world. I think they have changed their tune recently, especially since they have been making nuclear weapons. They realize now that it is possible with nuclear weapons to eliminate every single Chinese. Furthermore, the Chinese had reasoned that since nuclear weapons were especially effective against industrial concentrations, the United States and Europe would be more vulnerable than China. However, I think they are beginning to realize that their hard-won industrial gains are relatively more valuable to them than our industry is to us.

Now, the curious thing that has happened is that, with all this terror, there has been a balance of terror, a real one, between the United States and the Soviet Union at least. Both countries have come to realize that nuclear war cannot be an instrument of national policy. It's just unthinkable. The terrible thing about the current antiballistic-missile (the rocket designed to knock down a rocket) race is that the balance achieved over the last twenty years is being rudely and badly shaken. And if it is shaken enough, we may come to a point where indeed someone in a moment of panic or super-terror will say, "O.K., let's go, we have no other way out."

At the beginning of this lecture, I said rationality is not enough. And our nuclear confrontation is an illustration of that. It is an illustration of an ill-advised attempt to think our way through a complex situation by argument and counter-argument. Our society is a complex system. The nuclear confrontation is a complex system. And complex systems do not react as we imagine them to.

In that respect I would like to recommend a book which I think will be one of the great books of this decade, possibly of the century. It is *Urban Dynamics*, by Dr. Jay Forrester of the Massachusetts Institute of Technology. Dr. Forrester has simulated the life and death of a city on a computer, taking into account the hundreds of factors that govern the population, housing, economic behavior. The ability of the computer to handle hundreds of details in moments makes possible for the first time an analysis that reveals the complex behavior of the city.

Aside from the rightness or wrongness of his analysis in its details, he has shown quite clearly that simple cause and effect do not operate in complicated systems. They behave in ways one would not expect. He calls such unexpected behavior counter-intuitive. For example, he demonstrates that if you build low-cost housing in a deteriorating city, the standard of living of the low-income segment of the population goes down. Peculiar.

He also shows that complex systems resist change dramatically. Another example: if you institute large training programs for underemployed persons, you have very little effect on the employability of the underemployed segment of the population in the medium long run. We have an instance of that in New York in our More Effective Schools program where $10 million or about $500 per child was spent to upgrade reading, writing, and arithmetic. An analysis shows little improvement over a four-year period.

Although complex systems have lives of their own and seem to go on doing things regardless of our attempt to manipulate them, Dr. Forrester demonstrates that they do have critical points where change has wide-ranging effect. The trouble is that the change may be deleterious. Only by the use of powerful analytical tools such as those developed by Dr. Forrester will we be able to deal with complex systems. Intuition only suggests possibility. Rationality—human thought—if used alone, can lead us astray. One needs a blend of analysis, science, technology, experiment, and politics to deal with such problems; otherwise we are doomed to make tragic errors.

I have taken this discursion because Dr. Forrester's discussion of complex systems illustrates the unexpected results of our rash behavior when confronted with such systems. With respect to the cities, such rashness is rewarded with a stagnant and unattractive city, but in other areas its reward may be the end of society.

Let me go on, then, to the second topic: exhaustion. As an introduction, I will read a poem by Robert Frost, who was the poet laureate of the Kennedy administration. Frost's poem is called "Fire and Ice."

> Some say the world will end in fire,
> Some say in ice.
> From what I've tasted of desire
> I hold with those who favor fire.
> But if it had to perish twice,
> I think I know enough of hate
> To say that for destruction ice
> Is also great
> And would suffice.*

Frost was not predicting a new ice age, although we may have another one because of the reckless way in which we are using our technology. But the poem instructs us emo-

* From *The Poetry of Robert Frost*, edited by Edward Connery Lathem. Copyright 1923 by Holt, Rinehart and Winston, Inc. Copyright 1951 by Robert Frost. Reprinted by permission of Holt, Rinehart and Winston, Inc.

tionally on what exhaustion is. And, as a society, we may exhaust ourselves by producing more people than we can feed, clothe, and give automobiles to. In this century, unlike any other century, we have invented death control without population control.

You notice, I don't say birth control, because we have invented birth control which doesn't necessarily control population. Because of population growth, according to one calculation, on November 13, 2026 (incidentally, a Friday), when I will be a hundred years old, there will be so many people on the face of the earth that not only will there be no room to stand, we'll squeeze each other to death.

Dr. Heinz von Forster, of the Illinois Institute of Technology, published the formula for this calculation some years ago in *Science*. I extended the data for another hundred years to the year 2126 and discovered that, if the population were unchecked, the entire surface of the earth would be covered by a wriggling mass of humanity expanding out into space with the speed of light.

Long before that happens, something has got to give, or not give, depending on how you look at it. We must discover what almost every other mammalian species has discovered; namely, how to control our population size before starvation sets in. Birds have discovered the technique, too. Birds establish territories by nonaggressive techniques. One male and one female use a territory to breed. Other males and females which fail to establish territories do not starve; they can still forage, but they do not breed. That kind of control is found throughout the animal kingdom.

In human society, only certain groups have discovered

how to control their populations. Western Europeans found out how to do it, curiously enough, before the invention of the vulcanization of rubber. We have no controls in this country despite the most elegant birth control techniques.

Now, it is strange that the underdeveloped countries—the ones most needful of population control—resist using those techniques. Modern research indicates the reasons. Underdeveloped countries are agrarian. Individuals understand almost intuitively that if you do not have a son nobody will succeed you to till the land and to take care of you in your old age. This understanding has become part of the religious outlook. Additionally, such countries have high infant-mortality rates. So, faced with the low survival of children, one continues to breed to insure one's old age.

So it is against self-interest to limit one's family under such circumstances, and we see the persistence of behavior for which there is no longer any need. We have to find for the developing countries not new methods of birth control but new methods of providing social security and of reducing the horrible infant-mortality rate. Unfortunately, because of the persistence of behavior, such solutions are likely in the short run to make things much worse before they get better.

As I was saying before, complex systems do not react as we expect them to. We must make the kinds of analyses that Dr. Forrester has made for the cities and we must have the political courage to apply them. Otherwise, we may indeed doom our society by failing to check its population.

Let me go on to the third apocalypse. In the Western world, we have all but eliminated most infectious disease. Death rates from pneumonia, tuberculosis, and polio have dropped to almost nothing. To illustrate the changes that have occurred since I was a child, I would guess that at my age I am the only person I know who was treated with *bankes*.*

The elimination of infectious disease confronts us with another terror, because we are on our way to building a sterile society, bacteriologically speaking. And therein lies potential catastrophe. In a few generations, our children will have no experience with infection. Who has diphtheria today? Or whooping cough? Or polio? We are vaccinating against measles and mumps. Soon, perhaps, the common cold will go.

This drive could upset our eons-old protection against disease. Here's how. We have two kinds of immunity, one specific, the other generalized. Specific immunity depends on an infection with a specific germ, so that, for example, if you once have polio or are vaccinated with polio virus, your body builds specific protection against future polio infection.

We know little about general immunity except that it is stimulated by infections in general: the more infections of different kinds that you have, the better are you able to fend off future infections. And as we build that sterile society, we will have less and less experience with infection, and our general immunity will decline.

And then suddenly out in Bangkok, a little virus mutates—changes—and becomes a virus against which we have not been vaccinated. It finds its way onto a trans-Pacific jet to

---

* Yiddish, meaning cups that are applied to the chest as a counter-irritant for croup.

New York City, and we're in trouble. That germ can spread rapidly through our unvaccinated, unprotected population and kill it off.

If you think this is a fairy tale, let me remind you that in the lifetime of some people right here such an epidemic has already occurred. In 1918, a world-wide pandemic of influenza killed between 18 million and 25 million persons. So we may be building a biological trap for ourselves unless we're very careful. While we're developing vaccines, we must develop systems for recognizing bacterial changes and then rapidly going into action against them. Otherwise, we may have a repeat of 1918 or worse.

A second and perhaps less immediate threat of extinction arises from the potential manipulation of human heredity, which some wag has defined as your not having any children if your grandfather didn't. In the fifteen years I have been reporting science, there has been a dramatic increase in the understanding of the chemical underpinnings of heredity. The symbol of this understanding is DNA, an abbreviation of a chemical—deoxyribonucleic acid—which is apparently the repository of the hereditary characters of all living things.

DNA determines your eye, hair and skin colors, intelligence, size, and shape. The combination of DNA from your mother and father makes you you. In the last fifteen years, scientists have learned how DNA controls the chemistry of our cells. With every advance in science comes very rapidly today, on its back so to speak, the technology to use the information. One can imagine that DNA data will enable doctors and veterinarians and plant men to control the heredity of species. Part of this is very good: we can get better steaks,

16

more wheat, more rice. One can further imagine that doctors will eliminate deleterious genes from the human gene pool, so that if you have gout a doctor may, by pouring a little extra-special elixir on your sperm or egg, eliminate gout from your offspring. Possibly; I'm speculating a great deal here.

One could imagine further that one could affect I.Q. because I.Q. has a strong hereditary component. The time then is twenty-five, fifty, or one hundred years from now. A couple go to a physician and say: "You know, we didn't do very well. We couldn't get into City College because we only had I.Q.s of 100. Why don't you change our heredity so our children have I.Q.s of 150."

If the doctor had no medical reason not to do it, he would be hard-pressed ethically to refuse. Well, if 150 is good, 300 would be better, and soon self-interest would put us into an I.Q. race. What could happen under such circumstances?

An acquaintance of mine, Dr. Karl Cohen, was working at the Jackson Memorial Hospital at Bar Harbor, Maine, where they raise pure-strain mice who are as identical to one another as identical twins. Dr. Cohen wished to develop pure-strain rabbits. To do that, you interbreed them, mating father to daughter, mother to son, for many generations. It took thirty generations to accomplish the task in mice.

To speed things up and to give him greater control, Dr. Cohen bred the rabbits by artificial insemination. Along around the ninth generation, he discovered to his horror that he had created a breed of rabbits which could reproduce only by artificial insemination.

Now, in the laboratory, for the rabbit, that is only an inconvenience, but in the field it would be a disaster because, unless Karl Cohen is handy, no more rabbits. What I am saying by this example is that if you fool around with genetic material, you can breed into a population a maladaptive gene that could mean the extinction of that population with a change of environment, and one cannot really predict how the environment will change.

Breeders have known this for a long time. If you breed race horses to run fast, they end up with weak ankles; or cows to have large amounts of milk, they have udder disease. Breeding human beings for I.Q. could give us . . . what?

These are but a few examples to suggest that we live in a complex society driven by the twin engines of science and technology. For the future, we must consider very carefully the things we do to ourselves and society. In that case, every man should be a scientist to ask the right questions.

Are we going to put a nuclear plant in Ravenswood? Tell me what is going to happen to the radioactivity that comes out of the stack.

Are we going to have a vaccine against polio? What happens if the polio virus mutates? How shall we prepare for it?

Are we going to have a vast educational program called Head Start? How do you know it's going to work?

The answers to these questions should be in numerical terms—in terms that can tell you the likely outcome for the investment, so that you and I can be presented with choices for that investment. We don't want a system operated by computers that makes computers happy. We want to make decisions that will make people happy, keep them well fed, well clothed, and well housed.

We cannot answer these questions the way we have in the past. The method used so far is to get some articulate people together with some people with a lot of political power, and the most articulate fellow wins, evidence to the contrary notwithstanding. A new style of politics has to come to bear in which the electorate and government officials have to be presented with the kind of numerical analysis that enables them to make a real choice in a complex situation. Without that, we are doomed.

One last point. There is a lot of objection to science and technology. People say: we've had enough—nuclear weapons, rockets—enough. Let's go back to Thoreau's pond. I do not believe we can go back before we solve the very problems generated by technology. To allow things to go by themselves now is to allow the clock to run down.

The objections to science, however, are deep and never deeper than in those who have been brought up in the humanities rather than the sciences. Here is a little poem by e. e. cummings that illustrates that depth of feeling:

> (While you and i have lips and voices which
> are for kissing and to sing with
> who cares if some one-eyed son of a bitch
> invents an instrument to measure Spring with? *

Very bitter, good poet, but not very helpful.

Finally, let me say that I have spoken of these matters before, some time ago in New Jersey. I was then driving a

---

* From "voices to voices, lip to lip" in *Poems 1923–1954* by E. E. Cummings. Reprinted by permission of Harcourt Brace Jovanovich, Inc.

1947 Ford which had lost its first and reverse gears. To get to New Jersey from New York, I drove through the Lincoln Tunnel at rush hour and it was stop-and-go all the way. Then I stopped because the car in front of me had stopped. I looked at the gas gauge, which read empty. I looked up at the wall of the tunnel and there was a line running up the wall, one side of which was marked "New Jersey," the other "New York." As I was wondering whether I would ever get out of the tunnel, I thought the situation was a good metaphor for my talk.

We in the twentieth century have come through a very long tunnel—the evolution of the human species, the 10,000 years of human history, the one century of scientific achievment, the twenty years of excessive technology—and we have made it up to this point.

But we have a very long distance to go to get out of the other end and the question is: will we run out of gas?

When Synagogues Became Temples

MILTON HIMMELFARB

Director of Information and Research,
American Jewish Committee

One of the most interesting things in Dr. Perilman's kind invitation to speak with you this afternoon was what was printed at the top of the letter. Printed at the top was "Congregation Emanu-El." For me, as I think for most people, this is not Congregation Emanu-El, it is Temple Emanu-El. Similarly, across the park, the oldest Jewish congregation in the United States is not known by its official name, Congregation Shearith Israel; it is known as the Spanish and Portuguese Synagogue. Sometimes trivial things can open a perspective. Seeing your letterhead, I asked myself: "When did Jews start calling their synagogues temples, and why?"

That seems to be rather recent. As far as I know, the first synagogue to be called a temple was the famous Jacobson

21

Temple in Hamburg, the first Reform congregation. Of course, "temple" is not a Reform word, it is a non-Orthodox word. If you go about the country, you are just as likely to find that a synagogue calling itself temple is Conservative as that it is Reform, as likely to find Conservative Temples Emanu-El as Reform ones. What is important about Conservative and Reform is that both are non-Orthodox. That is the big difference—between Orthodox and non-Orthodox. The only Orthodox synagogue that I know of called a temple is the Tempio in Rome.

What need was there to call a synagogue a temple? Let me answer that question with another question. What need was there for Jews to call themselves Hebrews, or Israelites? Jews began to call their synagogues temples when they began to call themselves Hebrews or Israelites.

That was as true here as in Europe. George Washington's famous "to bigotry no sanction" occurs in his letter "to the Hebrew Congregation in Newport, Rhode Island." Neither the phrase nor the form of address was original with him. He was responding to a letter signed "by order of the Hebrew Congregation in Newport, Rhode Island," which expressed joy and "a deep sense of gratitude to the Almighty" for "a Government, which to bigotry gives no sanction." The congregation was Sephardi. It was also Orthodox—there was no other kind of Judaism then. We can understand why the signer, Moses Seixas, did not use the formal name of his congregation, Jeshuat Israel (the Salvation of Israel). But why did he say Hebrew Congregation? Why not Jewish Congregation?

Or again, the first nation-wide organization of Jews in

America, more than a hundred years ago, was the Board of Delegates of American *Israelites*. This congregation belongs to the Union of American *Hebrew* Congregations. Your rabbis were educated at the *Hebrew* Union College. Nor is this German Jewish (and old-American Sephardi), as opposed to East European Jewish. The *Hebrew* Immigrant Aid Society was an East European institution. It seems that the first institution in the United States to call itself Jewish, after the Colonial period, was the Jewish Theological Seminary, established in 1886, with the Jewish Publication Society and American Jewish Committee following suit.

The answer is not far to seek. Just look at how the big dictionaries define "Jew." In Western culture, "Jew" was a dirty word. It had far less to do with a religion, a tradition, a culture, a historical people, than with unpleasant personal characteristics and a revolting commercial morality. "Jew" meant swindler, usurer. This was not the arbitrary decision of the scholars who compiled those dictionaries. Going through literature to see how words had been used, the scholars discovered that, both for the folk and for the greatest writers, "Jew" meant those things.

Now the whole point about modern Jews was that they wanted to draw a sharp distinction between themselves— the modern, one might say the civilized, Jews—and the other kind of Jews. The moderns disapproved of the old-fashioned Jews' ways of worship, of living in society, of making a living. To distinguish themselves—and it was necessary to distinguish themselves—they called themselves Hebrews or Israelites, and their synagogues temples.

Of course, the old-fashioned word for synagogue was not

synagogue, either. It was school: in Yiddish *shul*, in German *Schul(e)*, as in Prague the famous *Altneuschul*, and even in Venice *la scuola*, "the school." "Synagogue," which does not occur in the Jewish Bible, is frequent in the New Testament. In Luther's version, the foundation of Modern High German, the Greek *sunagōgē* (when it means the Jewish institution) is always *Schule*; for example, *sunagōgē toû satanâ*, "synagogue of Satan," is *des Satans Schule*.

Shul is, for the Hebrew, *bet midrash*. A *bet midrash* is where you study, where you learn. *Bet keneset* is a place of assembly: *sunagōgē*, literally, is "assembly." The more common term is *bet midrash*.

What is bad about calling synagogues schools? "School" sounds educated, it sounds—as some of us used to say—refined. The answer is that *shul* does not sound at all refined. Once, in the high school I went to, a German was a minute or two late in entering the classroom where he taught German. When he found the students—as was natural—horsing around, he exclaimed: *"Was ist das, eine Judenschule?"* He may not even have been conscious that most of the students were Jews. *Judenschule* is good idiomatic German for noise, disorder, lack of decorum. When Jews who wanted to think of themselves as proper and gentlemanly came to give a name to their institution, they had to show how different their new kind of synagogue was from the old kind. The old kind was a shul. The new kind would be a temple.

But why temple, why not synagogue? After all, old-fashioned Jews had no more called a shul a synagogue than a temple. I think there were three reasons. The first is that in Western languages "synagogue" sounds alien and "temple" does not (and that New Testament phrase does imply that a synagogue is Satan's domain). The second reason is that "temple" was part of the vocabulary and symbolism of Freemasonry, which enjoyed the esteem of enlightened and progressive Gentiles, to which some of the Jewish modernizers belonged and to which all were well disposed. The last reason is that "temple" has, or had, a resonance for Jewish ears. According to Jewish law, only in Jerusalem are Jews allowed to have a Temple. To call a Jewish institution in Hamburg or New York a temple was a compressed ideological manifesto. It meant: "We are Germans (Americans, etc.) of the Mosaic persuasion. Not Palestine but Germany (the United States, etc.) is our Zion, and not the old Jerusalem but Berlin (Washington, etc.) is our new Jerusalem."

A hundred and fifty and two hundred years ago, when Jews were becoming modern, all this was historically necessary. But, as we know, everything has a cost. The cost of my being a man is that I am not a woman; the cost of my living in 1969 is that I did not live in 1869 and will not live in 2069. What is the cost of our having called our synagogues temples? By coincidence, we find the answer suggested in, of all places, the haftarah we read yesterday.

Yesterday the Torah lesson was Toledot, in Genesis: "Now these are the generations"—*toledot*—"of Isaac." It tells how the blessing that had been transmitted from Abraham to Isaac was in turn transmitted not to Isaac's elder son Esau but to Esau's twin, Jacob. Many of the stories about Jacob are what folklorists know as tricksters' tales. Jacob played two tricks on Esau by means of which, in the working out of God's providential will, it was Jacob rather than

25

Esau who received the birthright and the blessing. And here I cannot refrain from telling a story that bears on the dictionaries' inductive definitions of "Jew."

In those Tom Jones days when many Church of England clergymen were huntin', shootin', and fishin' parsons, one such parson was preaching to his congregation of yokels. His subject, precisely, was the story of Jacob and Esau, and as the parson told the story his indignation grew, until he concluded with this: "Esau was in the field, hunting, like the gentleman he was, whilst Jacob was skulking in his tent, like the sneak of a little Jew *he* was."

Now I open another parenthesis. The Bible seems to have an implicit principle not of primogeniture, whereby the eldest son inherits, but of ultimogeniture, whereby the youngest inherits. Isaac is younger than Ishmael, but birthright and blessing go to Isaac. Jacob is younger than Esau, but birthright and blessing go to Jacob. Jacob's elder sons do not get the primary blessing; younger sons do—Judah and Joseph. When the time comes for Joseph's sons to be blessed, Jacob deliberately reverses his hands and gives the primacy of the blessing to the younger Ephraim rather than to the older Manasseh. Moses is younger than his brother Aaron. David is the youngest of a junior family. Solomon is not David's eldest son.

There is an interesting theory about this—that the biblical *de facto* ultimogeniture reflects our ancestors' self-consciousness, or self-understanding. In the ancient world they were junior, just as they were inferior—in numbers, culture, and civilization—to Mesopotamia and to Egypt. Juniority became elevated almost to a kind of religious principle; and this is related to the traditional Jewish insistence on loving the weak, especially the stranger, "for ye were strangers in the land of Egypt." Jews have always believed that not to the senior, big, and strong does the blessing go.

Of special interest for our purposes is that of course that Genesis lesson is accompanied by a prophetical lesson, the haftarah. The haftarah is from Malachi, the last of the prophets, and the book of Malachi is read because of its beginning: Malachi, too, talks about Jacob and Esau. He lived at a time when the Edomites, the descendants of Esau, were bitter enemies of the Jews who had returned from the Babylonian captivity. Malachi is not fond of Esau, which is to say, of Edom. Right at the start he says: "Is not Esau a brother to Jacob? says the Lord, yet I have loved Jacob, and Esau I have not loved. . . ." But from our point of view the important thing is how the haftarah ends. Malachi 2:6 is as follows: "A Torah of truth"—an instruction of truth, the law of truth—"was in his mouth and iniquity was not found on his lips. In peace and uprightness he walked with Me, and he turned many away from sin."

Whom can the prophet be talking about? The "he" of Malachi seems to be a Messianic figure, like the one in the fifty-third chapter of Isaiah: ". . . by his knowledge shall the righteous one, My servant, make many to be accounted righteous; and he shall bear their iniquities." Having been so exposed to Christian culture, we may even be reminded of the Christian thinking about Jesus.

That was Malachi 2:6. In 2:7, the last verse of the haftarah, we learn who that Messianic figure is. Of all people, he is the priest, the *kohen:* "For the lips of the priest shall guard knowledge, and men shall seek Torah"—again, instruction, law—"from his mouth, for he is the *mal'akh* of the LORD of Hosts." Is *mal'akh* messenger here, or angel? ("Malachi" = "my [or My] *mal'akh*.") Malachi, the last of the prophets, thinks of the priest as being at least a messenger of God, and maybe an angel. "Every schoolboy knows" that prophet is the enemy of priest, prophecy the enemy of priesthood. Here is the last of the prophets making greater claims for the priest than the priestly document itself.

Between the end of prophecy and the beginning of rabbinical literature, Judaism accomplished three great religious revolutions, which make this priestly verse of Malachi obsolete. They introduce a new outlook, a new way of doing things.

First is that revolutionary institution the synagogue. It is not a temple. The meaning of the Latin *templum*, "temple," is much like that of the Hebrew *bet miqdash*: a sacred place, set apart. A synagogue is not that at all. The first religious revolution is that the synagogue, a place where one prays (and studies), parallels and ultimately replaces the temple.

The second revolution is a deliberate falsification of Malachi's prophecy: men do *not* seek Torah from the mouth of the priest; Torah is democratized. Ezra insists that Jews shall hear Torah all the time, he won't let them alone. He gathers them together and reads Torah to them. He suspects that some of them don't know Hebrew too well, so he has Torah interpreted for them: after each Hebrew verse is read, the interpreter gives it to the people in their language, Aramaic. Every Sabbath morning a Jew has to read a longish Torah lesson; every Saturday afternoon a piece of next week's

Torah lesson. Monday and Thursday are market days, when Jews are more likely to go to the synagogue than on other days. On Mondays and Thursdays some Torah is read in the synagogue. So, far from being the monopoly of a priestly class, Torah becomes the possession of the entire community. Torah is not esoteric but exoteric. The effort of Judaism is to make Torah public and thus to realize the ambition of the Bible itself, that we shall be a kingdom of priests and a holy nation. In a kingdom where all are priests, what special eminence is there for a priesthood?

The third revolution produces the new specialist in Torah. The verse in Malachi says that people go to the priest for Torah. What is the rabbinical literature that Jews know best, or anyway least poorly? Pirqe Avot. Malachi says priesthood and Torah are practically identical; Pirqe Avot draws a sharp distinction between them. Pirqe Avot says: "Torah is greater than priesthood and greater than kingship." As these are different from each other, so are king, priest, and Torah specialist different from each other. The Torah specialist is not a priest. If a priest is also a Torah specialist, that is a coincidence. How do you become a Torah specialist? The way in which Pirqe Avot describes the acquisition of Torah reminds me a little of the stories my physician friends used to tell me about how it was with them when they were in medical school and later when they were interns: "This is the way of Torah. You will eat a morsel of bread with salt, and drink water by measure, and sleep upon the ground, and live a life of trouble, and in the Torah you shall toil."

How do you become a Torah specialist? You do not get

it by inheritance; you work very hard. Just so, how do you become a doctor? You work. Torah becomes a layman's specialty, like secular law or secular medicine. What Judaism has done is to remove priestly leadership and substitute lay leadership. The rabbi is a layman, in this sense. He is not a priest, he is a Torah specialist. How did he become a Torah specialist? By the method that has been set out. He worked very hard.

These, then, are three of the great revolutions that Judaism has wrought in the history of humanity: the synagogue; making religious knowledge public rather than private; and making the distinctive religious personality not a priest but a layman. Obviously, these are associated with each other.

The Jewish reality fulfilled the ideal: Torah was lay, unpriestly. But a temple is where priests officiate. How curious! The people who first called their synagogues temples were Reform Jews. What did Reform mean in the context of its time? The Reformers were Germans. In Germany, *Reform* echoes *Reformation*. The Protestant Reformation is central in the self-consciousness of Germany; Luther is a central figure in the political and cultural history of Germany. When a German Jew spoke of Reform, he was invoking the Reformation, if only implicitly. But the Reformation was the Protestant revolution against Catholicism, against priestly authority. The slogan of the Protestant Reformation is the priesthood of all believers. Why, then, should the institution of Reform Jews—Jews who are, so to speak, Protestant rather than Catholic—be called a temple? A temple is a priestly, "Catholic" institution. It is the shul (or synagogue) that is the lay, "Protestant" institution.

May we explain this by the hypothesis that there is an inherent tendency in every religious functionary to try to become a monopolist? That would be a good, vulgar-Marxist interpretation, and we dues-paying members of the congregations like to make our little cracks about our rabbis. In fact, the real complaint that we dues-payers have against our rabbis is that they won't let up, like Ezra at the beginning. When we keep our children home from Hebrew school, or Sunday school, what is the classical phrase we use? "So he'll become a rabbi a week later." That fellow up there, the rabbi, is trying to kidnap my son and make a rabbi out of him. We do not suspect the rabbi of trying to monopolize religious knowledge, of trying to keep it to himself. On the contrary, we call him a busybody. Instead of respecting the division of labor, with him knowing Torah and us ignorant of Torah, he intrudes on our privacy and tries to get us to know Torah, too. There is the old joke about the brotherhood president's complaint: "Things have come to a pretty pass when a rabbi can't talk to a brotherhood meeting without insinuating religion into his remarks." The rabbis have never adjusted to this priestly division of labor, which we dues-payers created at the very beginning of the necessary Reform revolution. We said we were antipriestly, when in fact we were perfectly willing to re-create a new priesthood and a new division of functions: the rabbi knows, and we stay away. We hope the rabbi is happy with that arrangement. We know we are.

Why this should have happened is not hard to see. There *is* such a thing as the division of labor. No one can know everything. If I have to know tax law really well, how can I simultaneously know Torah well? Or if I am to be a nuclear physicist, how can you expect me to read Psalms in Hebrew?

But there is something else as well. Calling ourselves Hebrews or Israelites, rather than Jews, we created another kind of division of labor. We paid certain people to be rabbis and therefore to be—how shall I say?—the Jewish Jews, which would allow us with a better conscience to be un-Jewish Jews. There was that about us modern Jews which impelled us in that direction. Probably there was no way to avoid it, and the course of Jewish history would have been worse if Reform and all the other modernizations had not happened. The question is: is that direction still necessary, still inevitable?

We have seen that people are less likely to call themselves Hebrews or Israelites today, more likely to call themselves Jews, than a hundred years ago. In France, after World War II, a new Jewish communal institution was created, whose name is Conseil Représentatif des *Juifs* de France (Juifs = Jews); whereas the name of the Napoleonic creation was Consistoire Central des *Israélites* de France. After 1945 Jews could say, needed to say: we are Juifs, not Israélites. A certain chapter in the psychological history of the Jews had been closed, and a new chapter opened. It is hard to imagine a future Jewish institution in the United States, unless it is a Hebrew school, that will call itself Hebrew. It will be Jewish. Nowadays we can look almost as historians upon the Oxford English Dictionary's definitions of "Jew." "Yes, indeed," we can say, "isn't it interesting that people used to think of Jews in that fashion?" We are fortunate that this has happened to us—though to people of my generation it has not happened so deeply and intimately as to our children.

If this is so, certain questions must be raised about the institution that parallels Hebrew and Israelite, the temple. Going with priest, temple goes counter to the essential instinct and essential historical lesson of Judaism. It also goes counter to the needs of people today. These are needs of participation, of feeling that you make a difference, of community. There *is* a curse of bigness; individuals do feel lost. And there is a thirst also, it seems to me, for sharing earned authority—not authority but earned authority. The old division of labor becomes less appealing.

Dr. Perilman has an Orthodox colleague, a mile north and a little to the east, who runs a fine Jewish day school. Once this rabbi told me that many of the Israeli consulate people send their children to his school, because there, more than anywhere else in New York, the children will not forget their Hebrew. The rabbi went on to say: "You know, most of these consulate people, they're not terribly pious. I conscientiously tell those parents who want to enroll their kids in my school that this is a religious, an Orthodox school, and that we teach the children Torah and commandments. One father answered me: 'That's all right, Rabbi. You make a Jew out of him; we'll take care of making a *goy* out of him.' "

I think this division of labor was the unspoken Jewish social contract for two hundred years, but I think it may be coming to an end.

Allow me to be personal. When I hear certain sermons, I'm a snob. I ask myself why the rabbi should think he knows more than I about the antiballistic missile. If I want to know about the antiballistic missile, I go to a professor of antiballisticmissilology. From a rabbi what I want to hear is Torah. That he knows better than I.

In some concrete and yet symbolic way, we will have to act on our knowledge that just as the Hebrew-Israelite chapter has been closed in modern Jewish history, so should the temple chapter be closed. We must reinstate the old and central tradition represented by synagogue and, even more, by shul. Shul is where you pray and where you learn and study. Nor do its merits end there. Temple may be grander, but shul is warmer.

These, then, are some of the reflections that can suggest themselves when one looks at a letterhead and reads a haftarah.

When Yesterday Becomes Tomorrow

BAYARD RUSTIN
Director of the A. Philip Randolph Institute

America is in perhaps the most difficult period it has been in since the Civil War and Reconstruction, and we are in this difficulty for two reasons. First, we are in difficulty because we are opposed to any social planning except where there is an opportunity for financial profit. This is a society which faces all its social problems only in times of severe crisis. Second, from the founding of this nation we have divorced our values from our practical political behavior, and this has created what Gunnar Myrdal has called "an American dilemma." I should like to give some historical evidence to illustrate what I mean.

Let us look at our inability to plan ahead, our tendency to meet problems only when they stare us straight in the face in times of crisis, at which point, of course, they have become almost insoluble. We wait until black people riot in the streets before we realize that there is a racial crisis and that our cities are decaying along with the people in them.

Now I'll tell you something very interesting. For ten years A. Philip Randolph and I begged the police department of New York City to place a Negro at the head of the Harlem precinct. Such a move would, at the very least, have improved the dreadful relations between the community and the police in that area. Well, we worked for ten years and we were ignored. One week after the 1964 riot they made a black man the chief police officer in Harlem, whereupon some young people who knew that Mr. Randolph and I had tried for ten years to accomplish the same thing wrote me an interesting note. "Why don't you and old Phil Randolph roll over. Get out of the way so that we can make progress. Whitey doesn't understand anything but violence. You tried for ten years and they laughed at you. We upgraded Lt. Seeley with sticks and stones and Molotov cocktails." I'm here to say to you that this tendency of American society to face a problem only in times of crisis robs intelligent leadership of the ability to lead. And we shall be plagued by this.

Now to my second point. The Declaration of Independence was signed in 1776, and it said that all men are created equal, but this is precisely what the Founding Fathers did not mean. What they meant was that all white men who are rich are created equal. Black slaves in the United States in 1776 were not equal, nor were white indentured servants. These great democrats had no notion of "one man, one vote." They saw to it that only people who owned vast amounts of property could vote. You'll note that I'm not raising a color question here, not fundamentally, at least. The Declaration of Independence, of course, was a mere piece of paper—it did not delegate power. When in 1789 a constitution was written which *did* delegate power, all the problems of inconsistency of 1776 were compounded. They were no longer simply moral and philosophical but also political, social, and economic.

We have the terrible picture of Mr. Benjamin Franklin standing up at the Constitutional Convention and saying that in order to have a United States it would be necessary to reduce almost a million people to a fraction. Negroes, it was decided, are not people, they are fractions. Each black was counted as three-fifths of a man in order that the Southerners could have greater power in the House of Representatives. Such is our heritage of inconsistency between our values of equality and our practice of injustice. I am not denouncing the men who gathered in Philadelphia to draft the Constitution. They were making great strides over what existed in Europe, and it was a progressive movement—the founding of the United States. However, in order to understand what is happening today, it is very important that we truly understand what happened yesterday.

Now take, for example, a man like Thomas Jefferson, a man who also had his inconsistencies. He also tried to separate morality from political behavior. Mr. Jefferson was so troubled about the immorality of slavery that he wrote a note saying that he could not die peacefully unless all his slaves were freed on his death. Mr. Jefferson had separated the moral problem of slavery from the political problem. He was more concerned with his own soul than with the welfare of the slaves. I raise a simple question: why did not Thomas Jefferson go into the House of Representatives and put forth a bill for the elimination of slavery? It never occurred to him to do this, because he suffered from the dilemma which troubles so many Americans—separation of morality from politics.

The abolitionist movement is another example of my point. I happen to be a Quaker—many of the abolitionists were Quakers. Many were fine, upstanding citizens. They were on fire against slavery and that is good, but to them slavery was exclusively an immoral institution. They did not see that it was also an economic institution. Harriet Beecher Stowe, William Lloyd Garrison, and the others, marvelous people, but not very good when it came to politics. When the war was over and the slaves were freed, black people in this country said that in order to be free they must have some property—40 acres and a mule. "Help us to get some property so that we begin life as free men," they said. At this point, however, the abolitionists disbanded and there was no energy left for developing a political and economic program to support real freedom for the Negro. These good and moral people, not being able to see the economic and social implications of what they were demanding, went back to their churches, went back to their families, and permitted the Negro for a hundred years to remain in poverty and subjection.

Now you may wonder why I'm raising this, and I'll tell you. There are many guilty white liberals today who like the Kerner Report because it says that white people are racists.

If we are not careful, the Kerner Report can do great damage because it can be and has been interpreted to say that we define everybody in the United States who is white as being a racist. Now, if that is the problem, what we ought really to do is to line up every white person with a psychiatrist, and once he has had his racism exorcized, then we shall have solved our nation's racial problem. Yet we would have solved very little even if we could accomplish this unlikely psychoanalytic undertaking. The fact of the matter is that individual racism is not the problem. It is institutional racism that is the problem, and the Kerner Report failed in that it did not outline a social and an economic program for dealing with institutional racism. But here again we are going off on a binge of morality—"Oh, it's terrible that I'm a racist"—instead of dealing with the institutionalized social and economic problems which, if solved, would reduce individual racism to an irreducible minimum.

Now Negroes in this country had no real freedom from 1865 to 1954. The 1954 Supreme Court decision was the beginning of a new move toward justice for black people which has resulted in expanded personal freedom and dignity, particularly with regard to voting rights and free access to public accommodations.

But again, the American people who said, "Yes, black people have a right to use theaters, hotels, busses, trains, etc.," did not see that the economic conditions in the cities and the ghettos were worsening. At the very moment when there was progress toward civil rights for Negroes, there was deterioration in the area of economic rights.

Since the 1954 Supreme Court decision, unemployment

for blacks has doubled; it has tripled for teenagers, quad-rupled for black women. There are more black youngsters in segregated classrooms than there were before the Supreme Court decision. The housing situation is infinitely worse, with more rats, more roaches, and more ghettos than we have ever had before. Black rage is mounting because of these conditions, and black rage increases white fear. This is our problem and we must find a solution to it. Anything which is done to accommodate to black rage at the expense of white fear will make the situation worse. And any effort to deal with white fear without simultaneously solving the social problems which produce black rage will also make the situation worse. Black rage and white fear feed on each other, and they must be simultaneously eliminated, and this can only be done by an economic program designed to deal with both.

Now many Jews, as well as Irish and Hungarians, are constantly saying to me, "Mr. Rustin, we made it on our own. Why don't Negroes make it on their own?" That is an interesting question which I should like to deal with.

First of all, anyone who attempts to compare the social and economic reality of today with the economic reality of 1900, when his grandfather came from the old country, is making a great mistake. This is not 1900, or 1910, or 1880. This is 1969. But I don't want to leave it on that level. Let me be a little more precise. When the immigrants came from Europe there were a series of stair steps provided by the society to help them rise economically and socially. Let me never hear an immigrant's grandson say that his grandfather was not given anything. He was. Number one, there was still free land in the West where settlers could establish themselves. And I can assure you if tomorrow they were to give away Central Park, we Negroes would be the first ones there to stake out land, but they never will give it away.

Number two, when your ancestors came, many of them were uneducated people, but they could make it because society at that time was prepared to buy their muscle power and their back power. Today, in the face of automation and cybernation, you cannot sell muscle power. You cannot give it away. When your ancestors came, one did not need a high-school diploma. Today you do. You need skills, even a college diploma in most cases, and you can't acquire those skills when you are subjected to conditions of poverty and segregation. If there were today a mass emigration to America of people who had little education and could not speak English (as Negroes *can*), they would occupy and remain in the backwaters of our economy along with Negroes, Puerto Ricans, Mexican Americans, Appalachian whites, and many others.

Now, my friends, the only way we are going to get out of this problem is to build a new political coalition dedicated to radical change and the redistribution of wealth in this society. We may fool ourselves and have a "head start" and think that will solve the problem, or have "open admissions" in our colleges, which is another gimmick. Last year it was "decentralization"; the year before last, it was "the Allen plan"; the year before that, it was something else. We come up with one little gimmick after another because we don't want to face the fundamental economic problem.

In this city, unless we can get billions of dollars now for higher education, we *should not* have open admissions, be-

41

cause to bring in all these people without the money to make their education meaningful is to destroy education in the City of New York. And there are people who are prepared to do it. And they are prepared to do it for ugly reasons, because they want a cheap solution that will satisfy Negroes and get them off their wealthy backs.

We face problems today that none of your ancestors faced. There is, first, the technological revolution. And second, the proliferation of local governments and the emergence of metropolitan disparities. (How do black and poor people, white or Puerto Rican, operate in this exceedingly complicated situation?) Third, there is the concentration of minorities and poor persons in deteriorating slums. Fourth, we face the rising cost of public services in our cities. Blacks are not responsible for that, nor are Puerto Ricans. It is the nature of our time. Then there is the matter of a depleted tax base. The problem is in the city, but the people with the money with which to pay taxes live in the suburbs. They come in from the suburbs and make money in the city. They carry their taxes back to the suburbs. All the while, people in the city get poorer and poorer and poorer. We do not have the tax base for dealing with a single problem. Until the federal government is willing to commit the funds to solve these problems, the housing will get worse, crime will rise, people will go uneducated.

When your grandfathers came, there were not shifts in the location of industrial development, as there are now, with new jobs opening up in the suburbs, while the poor are trapped in the city. There were not then the distorted national priorities we have now. In 1900 we were not spending forty billion dollars for going to the moon. We were not spending forty billion dollars on some useless war in Vietnam. But even if the war were over, there would be no more money for our cities. There was no more money after the Korean War: why should there be today? We need a social commitment to deal with these problems.

What I'm talking about is a political coalition. At the present time we have a coalition. It is made up of Catholics, Protestants, Jews, the trade-union movement, Negroes, liberals, and the like. It is not a strong coalition at this moment, however. It is very capable of dealing with dangers where it is under attack. Its problem is that it doesn't have enough energy to go out and do a creative job. We can get very excited when Mr. Haynsworth is going to be appointed. We can protect ourselves from that danger, at least for the moment. But we cannot win the struggle for the money to solve our problems.

I would like to outline at this point a program which we must carry out if this country is not to be destroyed by racial animosity.

Number one, friends, we are only going to educate people in this society when education becomes a right, free of cost, and not a privilege for the rich. You may be able to pay for your children to go to school, but the majority in this country do not have the funds. We must spend billions to enable everybody to get an education.

Second, this society cannot get out of its dilemma without a redefinition of work. You cannot have a technological revolution (which means machines do the work men used to do) without a social revolution that will offset its effects on

43

human beings. Therefore, we have to redefine work. We must define studying as work and pay poor students to study.

Third, there must be a guaranteed income for all those who are too old or too young to work, or who are mentally or physically incapable of working. At the same time there must be full employment at decent salaries for all who are willing and able to work. There must be free medical care. There must be the building of new towns and the rebuilding of the central cities and there must be adequate housing for all. Now this is going to cost billions and billions of dollars, literally. We have the money. We can do these things if we want to. In 1941, when it looked as if America were going to go to war, the last thing anybody asked was what would be the cost of defending ourselves, or if it would increase his taxes. What we said was: "Hitler must be destroyed, for he is evil, and we will do it no matter what it costs." We should approach the war on poverty with the same attitude. "Poverty is wrong, we intend to eliminate it, it doesn't matter how much it will cost, here are all the resources. If we have to ration or increase taxes, we'll do it."

The dilemma of this nation is that we are not prepared to do that; but if we do not, we may as well give up. This is a call for the redistribution of wealth in this society. There will be no peace, here or in the rest of the world, as long as affluence and poverty coexist, as long as the United States owns half the world's resources and everybody else must live on the other half.

The program which I am proposing is not only a redistribution of the wealth but the securing of wealth for those who have. For poor people will spend the billions of dollars they will get; they won't put it in their socks. They're going to go out and buy things with it and this will increase the gross national product and production in the United States. So the rich will get something out of this plan, too. All will benefit. And the mental health of the country will be restored.

There's a special place for the Jews in all of this. First of all, people who have known thousands of years of suffering must be sensitive to the suffering of others.

The Jew, from my reading of Jewish history and culture, is truly unique and chosen, for he has been chosen by God to be His suffering servant and by that experience to obtain the insight and the knowledge to help lift the suffering of others. That is God's commandment to Abraham, Isaac, and Jacob. The question is: will they follow this commandment today? Politically speaking, this is to ask: will Jews remain in a coalition for justice, or will they permit a small minority in the black community, who are reacting to four hundred years of mistreatment, to drive them out of this coalition with anti-Semitic foolishness and confrontationism? Are Jews to permit their heritage to be destroyed by blacks who behave that way? I think the Jews have done absolutely right in saying to James Forman: "We respect Negroes and we will not let you come and demand reparations from us. What we have must be given because it is right. It must be given out of the freedom of our hearts." In the eleventh century Maimonides spoke of a hierarchy of charity, the lowest form being to give when asked; the highest form being that which removes the necessity for charity. That is not Rustin, that is Maimonides in the eleventh century. But in today's context,

45

that can be done only by the public redistribution of wealth, not by private charity. Furthermore, what I ask is not what Forman asks. I don't want your love, I don't want your affection, I don't want your money even if you offer it. What I want more than anything else is *zadukkah*. Only the Jews have a single word for both charity and justice. The only way that people in this society can have *zadukkah* is by the redistribution of the wealth. They will not have it if charity is given them by an individual, but only if the situation is created whereby they can themselves grow because the society provides the social and economic means for justice.

Now Isaiah has said we must be opposed to injustice wherever it is, but first of all in oneself. The Jews have made a great contribution to justice for black men. Israel is making a great contribution to justice for black men throughout Africa. That is your heritage. Live up to it! Let nothing tear you away from it. Let nothing or nobody compromise your belief in social righteousness as taught by Isaiah and Jeremiah. And let that belief manifest itself in action. Let us together build a just society.

Where Are We—Where Are We Going?

MARSHALL SKLARE
Professor of Sociology, Yeshiva University

Let us take inventory of where we are in the Jewish community and where we are heading. Inventory-taking is no simple matter. Even in a field as seemingly objective as business there is much ambiguity in placing a value upon such intangible but crucial assets as "good will." Thus it is to be expected that different people (and certainly different Jews) will produce varying balance sheets when the enterprise being appraised is Jewish life. Indeed, the very same individual is capable of producing different balance sheets depending upon the mood of the moment.

Concerned Jews are fond of minimizing Jewish assets, but a fair-minded accountant must begin by pointing to the matter of Jewish survival. The fact is that the American Jew has survived unto the second, third, fourth, and even unto the fifth generation. There have been those who said that it was impossible for such survival to occur in the United States. It is a matter of record that a famous European rabbi, the Slutsker Rav, delivered a speech here in New York City in 1900 to what is now the Union of Orthodox Jewish Congregations of America, stating that Judaism had no chance of survival on American soil. He maintained that all Jews who wished to remain loyal to Jewish tradition should leave America and return to Eastern Europe. (Perhaps you noticed in your newspaper that the Union of Orthodox Jewish Congregations has just concluded its most recent convention in Chicago.) And the opinion of the Slutsker Rav was by no means idiosyncratic. Providentially, the overwhelming majority of American Jews did not follow such advice; we know very well what happened to their Jewish brothers who remained in Western and Eastern Europe. In sum, there were those both in Europe and in America who felt that there was no chance of Jewish survival in America, that America and Judaism were antagonistic.

The first thing to be said, then, is that Jews have survived longer than even many of the optimists were prepared to grant. Next, Jews have survived without being a problem to American society. There were those who felt that there would be a Jewish problem in America. There were Gentiles who felt that there would be a Jewish problem in America and there were Jews who felt that there would be a Jewish problem in America. Less than a century ago, many established Jews were certain that there was going to be a Jewish problem in America. They felt that America would be inundated by Jews who would not succeed in making a living, who would not succeed in adjusting to the country, who would be a drag on the Jewish community, and who would create serious intergroup-relations problems for those Jews who were already established here.

These projections turned out wrong—all wrong. The East European Jew has not created a social problem in the United States. In fact, one might contend that if all minority groups were like the Jewish group, there would be fewer social problems in the United States. From this vantage point, the immigrant Jew possessed a culture which was highly "functional" in terms of the American environment. And the immigrant Jew was characteristically a person with great self-confidence and ambition. The pity of it is that these qualities were not widely appreciated by the established community— they are only now being indirectly celebrated in the outpouring of books appearing on the subject of immigrant Jewish life, particularly the life of the Lower East Side of New York.

This brings us to the third item in our inventory: the fact that the American Jew has succeeded in that process which is thought of as quintessentially American—the process known as social mobility, specifically the movement upward from one class level to another. Whether correctly or not,

America is thought of as the great land of social mobility. And no group has been more mobile than the Jews—the Jews who in the space of two generations have achieved a class profile that resembles that of Episcopalians, Presbyterians, and other such favored WASPs.

As the fourth item on our balance sheet, I would enter the educational attainment of the American Jew. If America is the land of social mobility, it is also the land of educational attainment where the belief prevails that every man has a right to as much education as he is able to absorb. From this standpoint, nobody has been more American than the Jews. Again, they have succeeded in reaching the level achieved by the most favored Protestant denominations such as the Episcopalians and the Presbyterians. And the Jew has achieved such parity in spite of the recency of his arrival as well as the discrimination which has been practiced against him.

The fifth entry on the balance sheet is that the American Jew has succeeded in all these things on his own terms. By that I mean that he has succeeded without concealing his Jewishness (although admittedly this statement is more true of the present than of the past). It would of course have been possible to move up the educational and class ladder, as well as to avoid being a social problem, but to pay too great a price in the process—the price of repressing or even denying one's Jewishness. But the American Jew did not do this. Indeed, we are living through a period (perhaps we are at the end of it) where Jewishness is being displayed as never before. One has only to think of *Portnoy's Complaint* to realize the Jewish assertiveness of the present era. The expression of

Jewishness being so abundant, it has given rise to a Gentile countermovement. And it has stimulated Gentiles to assert that they are Jewish in the sense that they, too, know the meaning of suffering and alienation.

Last but not least, there is the Jewish community. Not only have Jews succeeded as individuals but they have also accomplished the feat of establishing a Jewish community in the United States. To be sure, it is a Jewish community which is very different from previous models. And while Jews may bemoan the indifference of their fellows to Jewish communal responsibilities, to knowledgeable Gentiles the Jewish community appears as vital and powerful. They wonder how the United Jewish Appeal does it, how the B'nai B'rith does it, how the Federation does it.

All of the developments which I have delineated are magnified because they take place against the background of the Holocaust. We know that American Jewry was only seconds away from destruction. The prosperity of American Jewry, then, seems that much more wondrous because it takes place against the background of the destruction of the great Jewish communities of Europe.

II

If these are some of the assets on the balance sheet of American Jewry's immediate past, what then of the present? What are some of the problems looming on the horizon of American Jewish life—problems which are capable of turning a favorable balance sheet into an unfavorable one?

The first matter to consider is anti-Semitism. This is a

problem which most Jews thought was over-and-done-with. After the destruction of Nazism and the necessary readjustments after World War II, so great was the optimism that there was even talk of dismantling the network of Jewish intergroup agencies. By the early 1960's a consensus had emerged: anti-Semitism as an active force in public life was a thing of the past, discrimination was on the wane, and prejudice would gradually wither away. It was assumed that all decent men were on the Jewish side. If they were not on the Jewish side, at least they would not deign to make use of anti-Semitism. Furthermore, the notion developed in the Jewish community that what was good for the Jews was good for everybody else—that the Jewish interest and the general good coincided. You will recall the statement of the late Charles Wilson of Detroit—"Engine Charlie" of General Motors. He attained immortality not so much because of his fame as a businessman as because of his declaration that what was good for General Motors was good for America. And the mood of the Jewish community became quite similar: what was good for Jews was good for America. Thus, there could be no contradiction between what was good for Jews and what was good for the country as a whole. In short, Judaism and liberalism were one and indivisible.

As the seventies emerge, there seems to be a growing disparity between all these comfortable assumptions and the reality that surrounds us. It is the Negroes and their aspirations that have upset these dreams of ours. They have thus exploded the conception that what was good for Jews was good for America, or, to put a finer point on it, what was good for Jews was *necessarily* good for America. With this has come a challenge to the concept of meritocracy; namely, that one should be rewarded on one's merit and that power should be exercised—and status accorded—to those who are meritorious. It was on the basis of the meritocracy conception that the Jews presented their credentials to America, saying it was not a man's religion, not a man's background, not a man's heritage, and not a man's race which ought to be the guide of how he should be rewarded. Rather, it was his merit which should be decisive. Jews worked hard to have the principle of meritocracy accepted. And as the American ethos evolved after World War II, the principle did indeed seem to be well on the way toward establishing itself.

The blacks have challenged the concept of meritocracy, feeling that they cannot succeed if merit is to be the principle by which rewards are to be distributed. This stance of theirs works to undercut the ground on which Jewish advance has proceeded. And the black revolution has gone even further: it has challenged the concept of the Jews that they could function as an elite group in American society. Thus, the Jews grew to conceive of themselves as a middle- and upper-class group serving an undifferentiated or general public, a public necessarily made up of a plurality of lower-class Gentiles. That the Jews, who started out in America from such humble beginnings, could hold such a conception is a tribute to their culture, their self-confidence, and their ambition.

Negroes have effectively challenged the concept that they should be served by a white elite. They prefer to be served by a black elite. With this has come a challenge to the concept that Jews should constitute an elite group serving Gentiles, especially Negro Gentiles. One has only to look at the school system in New York City, and the black challenge to the Jewish role in that system, to realize the implications of this challenge. And one only has to look at the encouragement by the WASP establishment to the decentralization effort to see that it can no longer be assumed that all decent men are on the Jewish side. Finally, the decentralization effort makes it even more difficult to maintain that Judaism and liberalism are one and indivisible, that what is good for Jews is also necessarily good for America.

If we must contend with new problems of intergroup relations, there are complementary problems of intragroup relations. I believe that it can be said that we now have a problem of intragroup relations the likes of which we have not known for some time, certainly since the establishment of the State of Israel. Before its establishment, there was a split in the Jewish community between the overwhelming majority who favored the establishment of some kind of a state and the relatively small anti-Zionist minority which opposed such a development. As the State of Israel became more firmly established, and as the Jewish position in America became more secure, that minority became ever smaller. Though the American Council for Judaism continued as an organization, its vigor declined. One could make the assumption that all Jews could be counted to stand together for those things which seemed to most people to be in the Jewish interest.

At the present time this sense of unity, this sense of cohesion, this sense of respect for one another, and this sense of confidence in one another, seem to be withering away. The problem is highlighted in New York City, where everything at the extreme ends of the Jewish spectrum is cast into bolder relief than elsewhere in the country. In New York City there is a split of unparalleled proportions in the Jewish community. This split was dramatized by the last mayoralty election and confirmed in a recent public-opinion poll about Jewish attitudes toward Negroes. The split is between richer Jews and poorer Jews, or, perhaps more correctly, between those who identify with richer Jews and those who identify with poorer Jews. It is also between those who are rich in education and those who are poor in education, and between those who are young and those who are old. All these divisions are reminiscent of the immigrant era when there were established Jews and newcomer Jews, uptown Jews and downtown Jews, German Jews and East European Jews. At that time two Jewish communities confronted each other across a wide barrier consisting of class, status, and power differences as well as religious and cultural distinctions.

In a sense, we are now reliving these painful old divisions. It can no longer be assumed that all Jews will have a common definition of what the Jewish interest is (or indeed that they are even prepared to identify and promote a distinctively Jewish interest). Jews who occupy different class positions, who have different educational attainments, who have different brow-levels see the Jewish interest differently. All this is in contrast to the situation in the immediate past. Then, for example, the most upper-class member of the German Jewish group as well as the most recently arrived and proletarian immigrant from Eastern Europe could both follow the

55

banner of Herbert Lehman. Lehman was able to span the distance between Park Avenue and Pitkin Avenue without being untrue to either.

Connected with this issue is the problem of recognizing and accepting the existence of anti-Semitism. Earlier generations of American Jews had no difficulty recognizing and accepting anti-Semitism. As the story once had it, this tendency of theirs extended even to charging anti-Semitism when a stutterer who was Jewish applied for a job as a radio announcer and was summarily rejected. If at one time some Jews were paranoid on the subject of anti-Semitism, there is at present quite the opposite phenomenon: the tendency to deny the existence of anti-Semitism.

However, some of those who are willing to concede the existence of anti-Semitism betray as dangerous a symptomatology as those who deny its existence, for they trace its prevalence to Jewish behavior. Younger Jews who are the products of more acculturated and privileged homes thus tend to trace Negro anti-Semitism to the behavior of Jewish slumlords and storekeepers. Trying to locate the cause of anti-Semitism within the Jewish group itself is not only fraught with methodological errors, but it has the most dangerous kind of psychological implications for the individual who engages in it. Indeed, it may eventuate in that most dangerous of emotions: self-hatred.

Next, there is the problem of attitudes toward Israel. This question is all very new—as we noted, by the early sixties what anti-Israel sentiment remained in the Jewish community was withering away. Now, however, the old anti-Zionism has been replaced by anti-Israel sentiment among younger

Jews of the New Left. Such sentiment is not concerned, as the old anti-Zionism was, with Jewish loyalties being in conflict with American loyalties. Rather, it accuses Israel of being an imperialist nation, and of being the worst kind of imperialist nation—one which is allied with the United States. Thus, in a sense, it is the reverse of the old anti-Zionism which maintained that Israel would diminish, or appear to diminish, the loyalty of the American Jew to America. In this new version, if Israel was anti-American, then it would deserve the support of the Jewish community.

This example of current anti-Israel sentiment is another painful illustration of how difficult the times are: Jewish interests and general interests do not seem to coincide as they appeared to have done in the past. Some Jews are, then, forced into a painful choice. Lacking a strong sense of Jewish identity, they cannot bring themselves to give Jewish interests priority. Rather, they are forced to justify their non-Jewish (or even anti-Jewish) choice by maintaining that the Jews have engaged in profiteering in the American ghetto or in being imperialists in the Near East. The Jews, thus, have left decent men no choice but to move away from them.

III

These are some of the debits in the current Jewish ledger which need to be balanced against the credits we reviewed at the outset. We must now turn to a more detailed consideration of the issue we have just noted: the problem of Jewish identity. At the present time it is this problem which constitutes the focus of concern for thoughtful Jews.

The first item that people generally place on the identity agenda is the threat of intermarriage. But let us move away from this familiar approach and look at identity from a more basic perspective. If we do, the immediate problem which confronts us is the erosion of Jewish culture. By "culture" I mean of course all those things that go into the way of life and the thought-patterns of the individual. In a word, the culture of the Jew has become less Jewish. It has become more general, which is to say more Gentile.

Since the cold weather is fast approaching, let us consider the case of the winter vacation. Miami Beach as we know it today is an American-Jewish creation—Jews were decisive in its development and accordingly have left the impress of their culture on Miami Beach. But for quite some time the world of the vacationing Jew has not been confined to Miami Beach: the Caribbean became the new frontier about two decades ago (now winter-vacation horizons extend even farther). However, a vacation in the Caribbean is not the same as a vacation in Miami Beach. Even if the vacationer spends all his time with other Jews, even if he takes the trouble to visit the local synagogue, and even if he restricts himself to foods that are permitted by Jewish law, he is surrounded by the culture of the American and the international hotel, the culture of the native population, and, finally, the culture of the European powers that were once predominant in the area. He may return to Brooklyn happy to be back in his accustomed environment, but he is not quite the same person —and the same Jew—that he was when he spent all his time on Lincoln Road. And what holds true here applies in a thousand and one other aspects of life.

When cultural dilution is severe enough, we may encounter the phenomenon of what a distinguished Jewish historian once called "inverted Marranism"—the state of being a Jew on the outside and a Gentile on the inside. While the Marranos of old were forced to display their Gentileness on the outside, they preserved a feeling of Jewishness on the inside. By way of contrast, the inverted Marrano proudly displays his Jewishness for all to see, but on the inside he is very much a Gentile. The phenomenon is of course well known among Negroes, who call such individuals "Oreos." The cookie is surely familiar to you.

Because of the erosion of Jewish culture, we also find in the Jewish group a less extreme phenomenon: young people who must be called underprivileged; Jewishly underprivileged, that is. They are in fact privileged in every way other than in their exposure to Jewish culture; they have every advantage but the advantage of a superior Jewish background. They have no handicaps but the handicap of Jewish illiteracy.

How did the erosion of Jewish culture occur? One important factor was the process which we analyzed earlier: social mobility. One of the results of the phenomenal rate of upward social mobility among Jews was that they lost much of their culture in the process of moving from the lower class to the middle class and, for some, to the upper class. The culture which they lost, or which became diluted, was Jewish culture; the culture which they adopted was the culture of the American middle class or upper class. (To be sure, in many cases their new culture was combined with a variety of Jewish elements.) We must conclude, then, that whatever the blessings which social mobility brought, and they were many, it brought deprivations as well. It speeded up the erosion of traditional Jewish culture. By integrating Jews into the culture of their new class-groups, it made difficult if not impossible the development of a new Jewish culture. In sum, mobility gravely complicated the problem of Jewish identity.

Secular education is another example of a blessing which brought deprivation as well. While a proclivity for education made Jews an American success story—and even suggested that they might serve as models for other groups—such education had a disorienting effect on Jewish identity, particularly since exposure to secular learning took place without the countervailing force of an equivalent Jewish education. The constantly growing margin between general education and Jewish education soon became a chasm. It has remained very wide in spite of efforts to intensify and upgrade Jewish education.

At one time the higher learning to which Jews were exposed occurred most often in the setting of institutions in which Jews were a majority and where Jewish culture had made an impress. Thus, in 1935 some 53 percent of all Jewish youth attending college were enrolled in New York City institutions, the great majority in the colleges that now make up City University. By 1963 this figure had fallen to 27 percent. At the present moment the figure is probably in the neighborhood of 20 percent and there is every likelihood that it will be reduced considerably in the near future. All of which is to say that Jewish youth are being spread much more widely throughout the American university system. It follows then that no longer is a significant percentage being educated in institutions that are dominated by Jews. Furthermore, the culture of the institutions which Jewish young people presently attend does not have a strong Jewish component. If you will, here is another case of the shift from Miami Beach to the Caribbean.

One cannot leave this subject without remarking on the campus revolution and Jewish youth. The campus revolution is, of course, a revolution that is centered in privileged campuses and it is felt most keenly by privileged youth who attend the more privileged schools. Therefore, it involves Jews. And since it is especially appealing to those who come from homes that are not only privileged but liberal, it necessarily involves Jews.

From the vantage point of Jewish identity, the significant thing about the campus revolution is that there is no connection between it and Jewish concerns. Jewish youth who participate (and so many do in one way or another) are involved in a cause that is much larger than the Jewish community, for the revolution is indeed world-wide. Such participation is in contrast to the campus radicals of an earlier generation that was taking part in a cause which had a definite Jewish purpose, whether recognized or not. It was natural that Jewish radicals then outnumbered Gentile radicals, something which no longer holds true. And since the present campus revolution has no connection with Jewish identity, participation in it constitutes a threat to Jewish continuity. Indeed, unconsciously, small circles of Jewish students have

61

recognized this fact and have sought to establish radical societies which have Jewish purposes, including that of challenging the so-called Jewish Establishment.

One cannot leave the subject of Jewish identity without a word about that institution which has been the subject of so many fictional, or should one say autobiographical, treatments: the Jewish family. Whatever the shortcomings of the Jewish family in the past, especially from the psychological standpoint, it did a passable job of transmitting identity. But even if one were to advance the claim that the present-day Jewish family presents a more wholesome emotional atmosphere than the old Jewish family, it would be difficult to maintain that it functions as well in the task of transmitting Jewish identity. Part of the reason for this shortcoming is that it is now in greater competition with the youngster's peer group and with a much more pervasive and distinct youth culture. Added to this situation is the fact that the parent no longer has as much Jewish culture to transmit as before. Thus, the survivalist forces in the Jewish community face the prospect of having to supplement the Jewish family —even, more radically, of having to replace the Jewish family. There is the stark fact, however, that no other social institution is capable of doing the job of building identity as naturally, economically, and efficiently as the family. It is no easier to replace the Jewish mother than it is to find a substitute for the Negro father.

We have seen that the American Jew has been a success: he has survived as a Jew, he has moved up the class and educational ladders with a speed that nobody in the established community—whether Jewish or Gentile—thought possible. He has succeeded in participating in American culture on his own terms and in building an organized Jewish community in the United States. But these trends are offset by the fact that Jews are now being confronted with problems of intergroup relations which so many thought would never be encountered again on American soil. Furthermore, there are emerging strains in the relationship between Jew and Jew highly reminiscent of an earlier era of American-Jewish history. And overall there is the fierce problem of Jewish identity, an issue which in part has emerged so forcefully just because Jews have climbed so successfully. There is a new breed of Jewishly-underprivileged young people whose situation is all the more poignant because they are blessed with so many other advantages. Finally, old mechanisms for building identity, notably the Jewish family, are much less efficient today than they were in the past.

It is apparent—I think—that in the immediate future the price of being a Jew is going to be much higher than before. Until this point, the cost was nominal. A minimal Jewish education sufficed for the second generation. It was possible to remain Jewish and at the same time to participate extensively in the general culture. The Jew was not forced into making choices between his liberalism and his Jewishness, or between his Jewishness and his participation in the general society. In the decade ahead, it is surely going to be harder, and much more expensive, to be a Jew than ever before. There is one consolation. If the price of being a Jew is on the rise, those who are willing to pay the cost will be in a position to appreciate their Jewishness all the more.

Creative Piety and Theology

KRISTER STENDAHL

Dean of Faculty of Divinity,
Harvard University

Dear Friends—or may I say: Brothers and Sisters in the senior department of what we Christians call the Biblical Community:

I feel honored that you have asked me to speak to you and to muse with you about where we are and where we are going. Lately—when dealing with rebellious students—I often get annoyed by the way some people say "we," as if they spoke for everybody, when they do not. So when I ask where are *we* and where are *we* going, I guess I should make it clear that I mean a Christian, a Protestant, a Lutheran "we." Or perhaps my *we* is ultimately just an "I"—"I" as a member of a badly troubled mankind, looking at God's world and Satan's inroads into that world through my windows which are partly European and partly filled both by a new love and by new feelings of horror about this new land of mine, the United States.

To speak on where we are and where we are going is to take inventory; it is a time for predictions. When the common calendar approaches an even thousand, there have always been groups who feel that the world is going to come to an end. Others just become conscious of a divide, of the end of an epoch. You have the option of counting according to the Jewish calendar, but even so, the year 2000 has a kind of magic effect on all our minds, our fears, our hopes, and our imagination. There is a good deal of prediction going on. We do not have prophets these days, but we have futurology —the study of the future by the help of computers and other means. The magic number 2000 makes us conscious of the future. We also live in a world in which we have come to see that we must calculate the effects of our technology on man and nature. We must know a little more about the long-range effects of what we are doing. So I take it that not only your anniversary but also the impending year 2000 is very much on our minds.

What about the future of Christianity? Seventy years ago, and especially in this country, there were great hopes as to the spread and victory of Christianity during the twentieth century. Many Christians are reminded of that hope weekly as they receive a journal that is called *The Christian Century*. That title reminds us of the fact that in the beginning of this century not only wild-eyed and evangelically zealous missionaries but average American Christians really believed that with a little help of God and a good deal of

American push in the missionary field we would by the year 2000 have a totally Christian world. Those who had a right and warm understanding for Judaism were willing to give it a place within such a Christian—or should we rather say Western—world. In any case, this century would be the Christian century, and it looked rather reasonable to many.

Statistics now indicate that at most the world will be 15 percent Christian by the year 2000. That was what became of the dream about the Christian century. That means that Christians will have to learn a new humility. We have to find in our hearts, in our theology, and in our actions a way to see how we fit into the plan of God as a minority—at least in a global perspective. It may even be that we have to come to our Jewish friends and ask how they do it. And I mean that more seriously than the rhetoric suggests.

So we are dealing with predictions—in the modern mode of futurology. The prophets of Israel were either fore-tellers or forthtellers, the textbooks tell us. There was a time when one really thought that the prophet was a prophet. He prophesied, he spoke about the future. But then it was recognized that perhaps they didn't do that only or primarily but that they were mighty preachers on political and social issues and mainly in the streets or in the temple. But the strange thing with the true prophets of Israel was that they were really neither forthtellers nor foretellers. They were the ones who with their words created the future. You remember the story about Elijah, that rather stern—who knows, perhaps even hippy-looking—prophet to whom the king says: You troubler of Israel! When he comes up against 850 prophets, that story suggests that those 850 had no power to create the future, but Elijah, who spoke with a divine insight, was really the one who had the creative power. I do not think that the Lord has given me that power. But I do think it is also true that a meaningful way of dealing with the future is to be aware that we do not just analyze it and talk about it but in that very process we are also creating it. That is the responsibility of church and synagogue.

In that perspective I want to address myself to three areas of Christian concern.

The first and most striking thing in Christianity today is ecumenism; that is, the urge toward Christian unity, and the bad conscience about Christian infighting over the centuries and now. Actually, we have come to a point where ecumenism, Christian unity, is more or less a fact in the minds of thoughtful and sensitive believers. The denominations and the organized churches may be dragging their feet, but theoretically and at the heart level the problems are solved. And the true divisions within Christianity today are not between Methodists and Congregationalists, or even Roman Catholics and Protestants, but are drawn right through these denominations in shades and types of traditionalism versus rejuvenation, liberalism versus conservatism, theologically and politically and otherwise. Whatever the organizational structure is, I think it has to be recognized that the feeling and the awareness in Christendom of a basic unity is far stronger than any division. One of the factors that led to that stage of affairs was an exegetical and Biblical principle—actually a rabbinic principle that Jesus also makes use of—which says: "But from the beginning it was not so."

As the rabbis had already started to do before the time of

Jesus, one looked back to the earlier and basic parts of the Torah. They were somehow closer to God, closer to the time of the Patriarchs. More of divine power had rubbed off on those of early times than on the later ones. "But from the beginning it was not so." And that perspective is very liberating in a religious community, and also in Christianity. The fact is that there was a time when many of those things which people now identify with Christianity just were not there yet. In that perspective, we are reminded of the fact that there are really no references to the Trinity in the New Testament. There are really no elaborate theologies of the kind we are familiar with today. These are leftovers from the long tradition of Christianity as it has built up; now and then it is refreshing to look back and to see that from the beginning it was not so. That is what liberates any tradition from the overweight of accumulated wisdom. A tradition can accumulate so much wisdom so that it gets loaded down by it. The wisdom may be great, but somehow the basic truth and experience can become hidden and even forgotten in the process. That is why we need the perspective: "But from the beginning it was not so." Such a simplification of the faith is very much involved in the new climate of ecumenism.

Such developments have much bearing on the relation between Judaism and Christianity. The more one studies the very early history of the relation between Judaism and Christianity, between Jesus and his opponents, between Paul and the Jewish communities around the Mediterranean and the first few generations of the Christian movement, the more, I think, it becomes clear that something went wrong. Somehow the disappointment among the Gentiles who loved Jesus, and perhaps even more among the Jews who believed that Jesus was the Messiah, was spilling over into a resentment, and ultimately the resentment hardened into anger and even hatred, which is ugly and which has left its mark on Christianity. It is understandable but it is ugly, and it seems that the time has come for a new try at understanding and redefining the relationship between Judaism and Christianity. It is important to note that many of the allegations traditionally made from the Jewish to the Christian community, and from the Christian to the Jewish, appear wrong. One of the most important additional factors here is what I would like to call just plain psychological insight. Once we really begin to understand the scapegoat mechanism in social psychology, the need for a minority to become the scapegoat for one's own guilt and frustrations, then we might be able to tackle this question theologically and spiritually in a new way.

We should also note that ecumenism within Christianity and the redefinition of the relation between Judaism and Christianity may also lead closer to a new understanding both in Judaism and in Christianity of the relation to other religions; if God is God and if we need that Word, then we need—and we need badly—a way to figure out what the ultimate plan of God is as to the various religions in an ever-shrinking world.

The second area of concern in contemporary and future Christianity is expressed by the catchword "God is Dead," a slogan well publicized by the news media and *Time* magazine, etc. It is strange indeed that theologians should use terms and language of that sort. But if one looks a little closer, it becomes clear that such slogans are what is meant when it is said that much traditional religious language has become obsolete, that the word God needs to be purified from false expectations and connotations. One could say that this slogan is a modern edition of the Mosaic commandment against man-made images of the one true and invisible God. What one seeks is to let religious experience here and now have a bigger voice and more impact in our telling what we mean when we say that we believe.

There are two kinds of religious language. There is what we call, in learned terms, theology in the *indirect* discourse, and there is theology in the *direct* discourse. In the former mode we say that the Christian answer, or the Christian truth, is so and so. But if you ask such a Christian spokesman: What do you think? How would you phrase it without hiding behind the tradition?—then the theology shrinks. Then we may get a mini-theology. One of the things that are happening in Protestant and Catholic theology today is a new inventory of what religious experience today actually suggests. There is a tremendous welling up of religiousness in this time of ours. Much is said and written about secularization and the world getting more secular, and that is perhaps true about the churches, but what we often fail to note is the immense religiousness especially of the younger generation. What I would call a metaphysical hunger. To be sure, it takes very strange expressions.

Astrology is getting big. You say: that just is not religion; but the funny thing is that people's ways of dealing with the Aquarian Age and all this kind of thing are not too different from the way in which people have always treated religion. There may be something to it somehow, but you wouldn't really dare to say that you really believed in it. You flirt with it, as most of us have a tendency to flirt with our own tradition and with our own faith. My predecessor at Harvard, Professor Arthur D. Nock, wrote a glorious study about piety among the Greeks in Athens in the fourth century before the Common Era, and on the basis of very good evidence he shows that an educated man didn't really believe in the oracle in Delphi and he knew that there was a lot of hoax going on, but somehow when the chips were down he went there. He both believed and didn't believe. And that's a little how many people these days flirt with astrology, just as they did in the Hellenistic era of the Jewish tradition, and before some of the astrological calculations had become sanctified through the power of the Kabbalah. In short, here is a sign of religious hunger, and when the churches and the synagogues do not satisfy the needs, the spiritual needs of the time, then the kids on the college campuses will import gurus from India and with or without drugs find satisfaction for their religious hunger. Our age is extremely hungry for religion.

And there is a new religious consciousness in youth culture that is seeking its own expression, and behind the beards and behind the four-letter words and behind the extreme violence of language, there is a strange kind of tenderness, a hunger for human relations, a suspicion not only of the military but also of the martial, and of the image of manliness. The long hair is another protest sign against the glorification of so-called male virtues. Here also is a hunger for tenderness.

71

Now these things work together, and if I read the signs right, there is a new *Homo religious*, a new kind of religious man, in the making. Religion is in for a comeback, over against the cool ways in which we have domesticated it within our social system. And behind the "God is Dead" language, I really hear the voice saying yes, we are enriched, we are inspired, we are guided by the tradition, but the time has come, as it comes from time to time, to speak our own language, to use our own symbols, to respond to the Torah or to Christ in direct, in primary, in our own language; and out of this will come renewal.

Such a renewal will give a new accent to our religious life. Up until recently the problem of man in general has been his powerlessness, but the most serious moral problem of today is that we have too much power. Power with the atom, power of changing the ecology, killing off the life of the ocean through the use of DDT which slowly comes down the rivers into the ocean. The very power of man as he manipulates his world has become so big that man's problem today is what to do with his tremendous power and his possibilities. It is not how to find power, or how to accept one's powerlessness. The checking of our power will be one of the concerns of the new faith. So that the "God is Dead" theology or language is really just a little bulldozer for new attempts to do the religious work and the religious thinking, and it will have its Jewish accent as well as its Christian accent but it will call for new thought and new piety in celebration and dance and all that goes with it.

And the third area within which we shall assess what is going on and what might be coming is, of course, the way in which the churches have taken to the streets; the new emphasis on social action and protest. Just as the Second Vatican Council was the watershed of ecumenism, and the "God is Dead" slogan pinpoints the new respect for religious experience, so the decisive event here was when Martin Luther King, Jr., called on the clergy of the land to join him in Selma, Alabama, quite a few years ago now. This was a decisive moment, and now any decent minister, rabbi, or priest should have been in prison at least once. A new style developed, a new angry, nonhumble, militant type of social witness which perhaps rocks the congregations more than anything else in the religious establishment today. This social ferment, this new kind of angriness, expresses a prophetic ideal, and just as in the story about Elijah to which I referred, the authorities and the establishment say in disgust and fear: "Art thou Elijah, the *troubler* of Israel?" And Elijah answers: "No, sir, you are the one who has caused trouble in Israel by established wickedness. Your violence is the greater one since you have the legal power to suppress and to enforce your interests through your courts and your police." That's roughly the confrontation that is going on.

Now this thing that is happening all around us when priests, ministers, and rabbis break into draft offices is felt by most of us as a total change in values, or if you want to be a little more critical than that, a total loss of values. But I don't think it takes too much of an analysis to show that there is not a single new value around. It is only that those in the social ferment, boys and girls, men and women, apply the old values in a new way and with a vengeance. Honesty, justice, concern for the widow and the orphan—for what else does the Lord desire than just these things? These are still the values. But there is a new way of applying, a new conscience, and behind it lie a few simple observations. One of the most gruesome is that most evil in this world is done by people who think they are doing good. I don't know if it has ever dawned upon you that evil is not very popular in the world. If a politician went to the people and said, let's be evil, let's drop napalm, let's kill as many people as we can, he wouldn't get much of a following. If Hitler had gone to the German people and said, let's be evil and let's just kill the Jews, he wouldn't have been a threat to God's people, he wouldn't have gotten such a following. But as it says in the New Testament that Satan transforms himself always into an angel of light, so it was then and so it is now. Somehow evil is always done in this world by people who claim that they are doing it for a good purpose, as even the Satanic acts of Hitler were sold under the slogan of national survival and "the final solution."

And ultimately that is true about all of us. Around Christmas time you will hear a lot of rhetoric about people of good will. I have never met a single person who wasn't. At least according to his own estimation. So there shouldn't be any evil in this world when there are so many people of good will. The real trouble with evil is that it is usually done by people who claim to be doing something good. That's the tragedy. And this is what the social activists in our churches and synagogues have seen and understood. Let me demonstrate this point in relation to "reconciliation," a deep and central theme of Christianity with many of its roots in the Yom Kippur. Reconciliation is a beautiful thing. I mean, who is not for reconciliation? I'll tell you too quickly who is not for reconciliation—the "have-nots." We who have plenty of things and power, we love reconciliation, we love peace and law. We do not want to be forced to give them up. A few minutes after Martin Luther King, Jr., had been assassinated, the TV and the radio and the press gave him a glorious and well-deserved title and from then on that title was repeated over and over again: Martin Luther King–Apostle of Nonviolence. And we nodded in sympathy and sorrow. But that night it dawned on me, as I heard it in a thicker, and thicker, and more emotional voice coming out of those nice white faces, that Martin Luther King's message to you and me was not the sweet word nonviolence—that was his message to his soul brothers and he delivered that message to them at great risk and price. To us he said: If you don't change your priorities and repent soon, you'll be in trouble! That was his message to us. But we'd rather bask in the warm religious language about the apostle of nonviolence because that sounds so much more dignified, so much more Christian, so much more religious. That's reconciliation for you! We love reconciliation since it is in our interest not to have too much trouble; we don't want to be blackmailed into giving up too many of our privileges.

If you have gotten a little of that insight, then you can see what a sick country we live in. Then you can understand some of the modern ferment among the young and how that fervor becomes so intense because they have lost the little hopes. There was that article in *The New York Times Magazine* a couple of months ago which said: You have to have been brought up in Scarsdale to know how bad it is. There is an awful lot of truth in that. The sensitive kids these days are the ones who have had it all, have seen it all, and they recognize that the little hopes of the American Dream are not enough to sustain them. To get it a little better through a little more education, move to a little better suburb, a little farther away from the dirt, and from the pollution—that just won't work. You just can't move that far. It is almost like in the 139th Psalm, which says: "If I make my bed in Sheol, behold, Thou art there." So you just can't move any more. The little hopes do not sustain the young, and so comes their guilt, their guilt as to why we were born affluent. We in the West, constituting about 20 percent of the world's population, live on 80 percent of the world's wealth and resources, and the other 20 percent of the resources are left to the other 80 percent, which we call the Third World. And that guilt is immensely increased these last weeks by the stories from Vietnam and Mylai, immensely increased by the situation in the ghettos. The little hopes having gone, that guilt builds up into a new consciousness, a new feeling among those who are sensitive and those who think about the will of God—there is a call for radical repentance. Now this is difficult, but it is a fact. A fact in our seminaries, a fact in our colleges, a fact in many places. Many of these young people have been looking around to see whether there is any place, any institution in the world in which they can place some hope, and some have zeroed in on the religious institutions, not because they are that good, but because somehow Moses and Jesus get through to them and they feel that they have allies in the prophets.

So there are these three things: a new and playful and creative piety and theology are on the horizon, the new ecumenism is here, and so is the social ferment; the social ferment which most simply means that the primary question of what is right and wrong has to be seen in terms of social justice and economic responsibility.

The way to assess whether this is a moral congregation is to ask how the board decides the priorities when it settles the budget. That's ethics. That is the recent, almost violent change from primarily individual ethics to corporate ethics to the ethics of the community. The values for such an assessment are not new. They are good old values of honesty, justice, and love, but they are applied in a new way. And in this social ferment I guess one pictures God as looking down from heaven seeing what really troubles Him and what really troubles Him is perhaps not our little personal and individual idiosyncrasies and sins. Don't get me wrong, I am not in favor of individual sinning. But the important point is that we need a new imagination when it comes to what is the will of God in the world of social and economic justice.

As I see it, these tendencies of which I have spoken will remain with Protestantism and with Judaism on this American scene into the twenty-first century. They are the ones that shape the future. They are the strong tendencies and they have the makings of a real reformation. Of course, while a reformation is going on, it is always a little messy. It is only in retrospect—in the history books—that it looks so beautiful and clean. That was true with the early Pharisaic movement, that was true with the Hassidic movement, that was true about the Protestant Reformation and the French Revolution and all the rest.

So we are in a turbulent and messy situation, but in my analysis it is a creative mess, just as actually the birth of a child in all its glory is not a very "clean" phenomenon, but we do not take offense. We rather rejoice in the powers of life. So there is future for God's people and God's plan and God's world, I think, and I think we are in a period of renewal with a tremendous upsurge of moral and religious courage and creativity.

When people ask me if there is a future for the Church, I am always inclined to answer, oh, yes, I am sure; but whether you and I will be in on that future, or whether it will pass us by, that's the much more interesting and searching question.

And that's how I assess where we are and where we are going. From time to time comes that phenomenon in religious communities which I like to call the change of crew. That's what happened with the upsurge of the Pharisaic movement. There was a change of leadership and a change of crew. And when Jesus cried out, "Blessed are those who hunger and thirst for justice, for they shall be satisfied; and blessed are the poor in spirit . . ." he was expressing thoughts and ideas that any good Pharisee could and did utter. But that was not the point. He rather announced a change of crew, and in his case one that was to include Gentiles—and as it worked out almost only Gentiles. It is as a member of that crew that I have the privilege of speaking to you. And I must recognize that we Christians who were once the new crew on the ship called the Kingdom of God, we have grown old. And there may be time for a new crew. We may see it being gathered before our eyes . . .

So I have no worries for the future of the Church, but I hope and pray that we shall all together be able to join that crew, lest God's ship sail on without us.

The Problems We Face

ABRAHAM KAPLAN

Department of Philosophy,
University of Michigan

I have recently been occupying myself with a study of certain aspects of the Hassidic tradition. There is among the Hassidic masters one with whom I have a sense of kinship; I think you will recognize why. He came to my mind as I was listening to our Rabbi's introduction—I thought of Rabbi Naftali of the city of Ropshitz. He once said about himself, "In distant places I am known as the Tzaddik, the saint, of Ropshitz; in my own city they refer to me as 'our Rabbi.'" Then a pause, and he added, "My wife calls me 'Naftali.'"

I see here among you some dear, old friends; I am pleased to be here and I am particularly pleased to be here in my own person, as I know each of you is here in your own person, without regard to the classifications and identifications which make up, whether we will or no, so much a part of our lives.

I want to talk about the situation of the Jew in the world today and tomorrow. Alas, I am afraid that I must begin by making clear that anti-Semitism is not merely a part of our Jewish past. I pray that it will not be a part of our future, but what part it will play in the future depends significantly, I think, on how courageously and wisely we are prepared to face the present. There can be no glossing over the fact that at present there is throughout the world (and the United States is not an exception) a resurgent anti-Semitism. That world philosophical congress of which Dr. Perilman spoke, where I enjoyed the association of Professor Rotenstreich, was one in which we had originally hoped to enjoy also the participation of a Jewish colleague from Poland, who at the last minute was not permitted to come and who, as a matter of fact, has since lost his university position.

So far, what I have said is that we have troubles; I would like to speak concretely about the problems that are to be faced and that I am afraid are too much glossed over still— as though, if we do not speak of these things, they will disappear. Anti-Semitism in Poland, in the Soviet Union, and in many other places restates themes as old as recorded history. I use my words advisedly. Let me recommend to you a rereading of the opening chapter of the Book of Exodus: "There arose a Pharaoh who knew not Joseph. And he said, There is in our land a strange people who have grown rich and powerful. If there is a war they may join our enemies; we cannot be confident of their loyalty." There are comparable passages in the Book of Esther. I sometimes think that, however vicious the contemporary anti-Semitic propagandists, they might improve their technique if from time to time they read our Scriptures. As least they would find a more eloquent language than they employ. It is distressing to discover that there is nothing new under the sun, after all. I hope that the time will come when it will be familiar only to the historian and antiquarian. But today it is not something to be found only in far countries; it is present here in the United States as well.

The overt and vicious anti-Semitic themes to be found today in the literature of militant blacks and the New Left and others is in no significant respect, I believe, different from the older materials, except, perhaps, in this—that there is something new stemming from the fantastic, wonderful, miraculous success of the State of Israel in maintaining itself in the face of intransigent opposition. There are people now who say, "We're not anti-Semites, it's just that we're opposed to . . ." I cannot bring myself to repeat the falsehoods and distortions which usually follow that kind of phrasing. It really is an extraordinary feature of contemporary political history that, no matter what political oppositions you can identify, there is one point on which you can expect to find the strangest bedfellows. All are united in their hostility to Israel and, by a very simple and direct implication, to the Jew—whether it is the Soviet Union or its bitter enemy, China; whether it is Pope or Panther; whether it is France or (fill out your own list, if you like, of the world's powers). If we stood in some alignment so that we could say, "Well, some people are for us and some against," that would be the very nature of politics. But that is not the situation; I would like this to be my first premise for any subsequent inferences.

I do not mean to say that discrimination against the Jew is a marked feature of contemporary life in America; it is not. We would be doing ourselves and others a disservice if we were to pretend that this is so. But I believe that we would also be doing a disservice if we were to pretend that there is no discrimination in practice, and even no prejudice in judgment or attitude. That, I think, is flatly false. Prejudice and discrimination are very closely linked to one another. Nowhere in human history has there been for any significant period of time a complex of prejudicial attitudes that did not express themselves in discriminatory action, just as nowhere in human history has there been a complex of discriminatory patterns of action that did not create, sustain, and reinforce prejudicial attitudes. I see no point in deceiving ourselves, or in deceiving others, with the pretense that really there is nothing for us to be concerned about. I believe there is a very great deal for us to be concerned about.

There is a special way in which prejudicial attitudes express themselves that is very hard to acknowledge, and even harder to protest against. It is what I call the poisoned sweets in human relations, the prejudice embodied in what the psychoanalyst characterizes as ambivalent attitudes—attitudes that are simultaneously positive and negative, wrapping up the poisons of the negative attitudes in the sweets of their positive expression. I will give you two examples, one with regard to the blacks, and one with regard to the Jews. Let me begin with the one with regard to the Jews; it is easier to see something in others, and it is more acceptable in others when we can see it in ourselves.

There are many people who imagine themselves to be speaking sweetly to us Jews when in fact what they are saying is fundamentally prejudicial, because they are not responding to us in terms of our own identities but in terms of our social identification as members of a certain group. I have spent some time on several occasions in Japan. Once the problem arose of schooling in Kyoto for my daughter. It was not easy to arrange; finally I found a school that at least used an Indo-European language. It was a French convent; the curriculum consisted of French, music, and mathematics; I was delighted to enroll her. A week or two later I received a call that the director of the school wanted to consult me. I was very happy to agree, wondering the while what my advice might be wanted for. Although I have spent my life as an educator, I have not had much to do with the second or third grades, and especially not with French and music, though I know a little mathematics. I thought there would probably be some questions on educational methods, curricula, textbooks, and the like. When I met the Mother Superior—and what a dear, sweet woman she was!—she chatted away about the school's building program, the problems of getting credits in yen, and so on. I was polite but wondered when she would get to the point. Gradually the realization dawned on me that she had gotten to the point. At last she said to me quite explicitly, "So you see, we have to make these long-term loans on such and such mortgages and notes. Usually we are advised on these matters by our friend, Mr. Goldberg. But he is now traveling in Europe, and so I thought that you, Dr. Kaplan, would be able to. . . ." If ever I write an autobiography this chapter will be called,

"My Career as Financial Wizard." That dear, sweet woman took it for granted that since I was Jewish I must be competent to advise her on matters of finance. I have been in other places, by the way, where some of my friends who are, indeed, financial wizards, but not professors of philosophy, were asked for their advice on philosophical questions; I think I got the worst of the exchange, but that is another matter. The point is that we respond prejudicially, whether what we are saying is positive or negative, if we deny individual identities and respond only in terms of group membership.

Another example I want to give, which some people might not find palatable, is this: there are many people in the United States today who deserve the appellation I heard somebody give them of "Tom Uncles." A Tom Uncle is the reverse of an Uncle Tom; it is someone who cannot bring himself ever to disagree with or be critical of anything that is said or done by a black. When a black expresses any attitude or belief whatever, the Tom Uncle says, "Yes sir, yes sir! That's absolutely correct!" I regard that behavior as a mistreatment of the black; it denies him the elementary right of every human being to be mistaken once in a while. (I was mistaken once; I remember clearly, it was in March 1956. My wife remembers even more clearly, though I am sorry to say that, each time she reminds me, it is a different date.) The point is that when we react to other individuals not as individuals but as members of some preassigned category, whether our reaction is superficially positive or negative, in a fundamental way there is something degrading in our response.

What I am saying is that we Jews now have a serious problem because more and more people are reacting to us as Jews, not as individual human beings, as Americans, as professionals.

Now I would like to say something about the ways in which we Jews over a period of time have responded to this problem; then I am going to talk about the ways society in general has chosen to deal with the problem; finally I shall draw some conclusions about what might be done, in my opinion, to further not only our personal values as individuals and as Jews but also our shared values as Americans and as human beings.

There was a time when we Jews responded to the prejudicial and often discriminatory treatment by encapsulating ourselves from the non-Jewish world, shutting ourselves off from it, reducing to an absolute minimum our transactions with the outside world. Often this was made very easy for us; sometimes it was the only alternative open to us. For two thousand years we were denied the possibility of living in freedom and dignity in our own land, as members of our own nation. That is the literal meaning of the word "goy"; it is not a term of contempt, but just means "nation." To be a nation has always been very highly thought of in Jewish history. One of the great promises which God makes to Abraham is that He will make of us a *goy gadol*—"You will *really* be goyim!" said He (that is, you will be a great nation). After millennia of a contrary history, we belong to a transitional generation for whom that history is very much a part of the present, while the present is not yet as deeply a part of a national future as I trust it will become.

Much of our Jewish experience is inescapably a reflection of the circumstance that we find ourselves in a non-Jewish milieu. My family and I were once in Bombay, where at that time we had no friends (we have since made many—Jews and non-Jews, Hindus, Christians, Parsis, Sikhs, Moslems). We observed Hanukkah in our hotel. It was quite a task to locate candles, and they were set, not in a silver Hanukkah lamp, but on the cover of a can of some kind. We felt we were exiles, strangers in a strange land. Then came an unforgettable moment. Through the open window of our hotel room we heard something that made us feel at home and that it really was Hanukkah, after all—on the sidewalk below was a group singing Christmas carols! We rushed down and showered the singers (evangelical missionaries) with rupees. To this day they must wonder where such devout Christians came from. The irony is that only hearing Christmas carols in the background, which is so much a part of our experience of Hanukkah in the United States, gave us a sense that it *was* Hanukkah we were celebrating.

We Jews can encapsulate ourselves psychologically; if not in fact maintaining the *stetl* culture (as anthropologists now call it), still living in a kind of mental ghetto. One form of such encapsulation is expressed in the notion that we can protect ourselves against incursions from the outside world by maintaining the unshakable conviction that everything Jewish is good, that there is no room for any criticism, doubt, or question of the significance or worth of anything Jewish.

There is a story that I know will be responded to by every father here, at least if he has a daughter. A young man comes to a father and says, "Sir, I would like to marry your daughter." (This makes it an old-fashioned story right away; there *was* a time when fathers were asked.) The father replies,

"Marry my daughter? You must be mad! Have you ever seen what her room looks like? Have you ever listened to her on the telephone? Did you ever see what happens to the kitchen when she cooks? Have you ever heard her argue with her mother?" The young man says, "Sir, I'm perfectly well aware of her faults." At which the father jumps out of his chair and cries, "Faults? What faults?" *That* is what it means to love. I need not entertain the absurd notion that everything of mine is so superlative in quality, in every dimension, that no question can possibly be raised about its shortcomings. We can recognize the shortcomings in those we love; and what then? The best of us is only human after all, and love does not hinge upon a weighing of virtues against faults.

Israelis have a line which even in these difficult days they use to express their basic attitudes toward their country—that they feel free to criticize Israel as if she had no enemies and to defend her as if she had no friends. I believe that this attitude is what is called for with regard to our Jewish identity—that we feel free to criticize the Jews as if Jews had no enemies and to defend the Jews as if Jews had no friends. God grant that the first "as if" becomes a fiction; I am afraid that today it is very far from fictitious.

There is a counterpart to this kind of chauvinistic refusal to recognize one's own shortcomings. It is that instead of saying that if something is Jewish it must be good, we say: If it is good, it must be Jewish. There is a lot of loose talk today about imperialism; here is a place where I think we really can talk about imperialism, but in a psychological sense, what I call *ego-imperialism*. In this sense, whenever the imperialist encounters some human achievement, he plants his flag on it and claims it as his own. The Soviets have really gone in for this ego-imperialism with their repeated insistence that every great invention and discovery was first made by a Russian; any day now I suppose it will turn out that Moses really came from somewhere in the Caucasus.

There is a game that I venture to say many of us have played. I am not going to describe the rules in detail; I suspect that you will recognize the game when I give you its name. It is called "You know who else?" One person says, "Did you know that so and so was Jewish?" and someone replies, "No, how about that! And you know who else?" thereby enlarging the shared imperialist domain. There is a kind of tribalism involved in this attitude, is there not, a kind of group egotism? I invoke a principle of Martin Buber's, that if something is wrong for an individual to do, it does not become right merely because it is done by the group. If there is something wrong in arrogating to myself all the virtues, it remains wrong, and perhaps becomes even more pernicious, when it expresses a generalized social policy.

I believe that the final collapse, from the standpoint of human values, of these unhappy ways of trying to cope with the pressures the world imposes upon Jews is manifested in the mechanism psychiatrists call "identifying with the aggressor," which we know colloquially as embodied in the formula "If you can't lick 'em, join 'em." There are, I'm sorry to say, many Jews whose attempts to cope with the problems of being Jewish take this form; they become what Horace Kallen once called *amateur gentiles*. They acquire only a negative identity. They find themselves, not in a positive content within the self, but in a bare, abstract, purely sociological differentiation from the other. The futility of this device for finding oneself was most memorably formulated by one of the Hassidic masters of the last century, who said, "If you are you only because I am I, and I am I only because you are you, then you are not you and I am not I."

I should like to repeat this profound aphorism not only to some Jews but to many blacks, and to many white racists as well. All of them make the fundamental mistake of supposing that they can find their own identities if they can reject the identities of others, achieve self-respect by showing contempt for others, come face to face with themselves if they turn their backs on others. It seems to me, not just from the standpoint of ethics but from the sober outlook of psychodynamics as well, that exactly the contrary is the truth.

There are a certain number of Jewish students—from my experience I am happy to say it is only a tiny proportion of Jewish students, yet the phenomenon is significant beyond their numbers—who have a deep contempt for themselves and who imagine that they can find themselves only if they identify with their aggressors and turn against themselves. A black student can stand up and say, "It is true that I have the privilege of being in a university. But I am not here to pursue only my own career, I see myself as a member of my people. The redemption of my people is not yet, and I hereby declare myself committed to the future of my whole people." Everybody will applaud, and rightly, at least the nobility of his purposes, whatever reservations they may have about his methods. But if a Jewish student were to rise and say, "Whatever my privileges, I am a Jew, a member of my peo-

90

ple. The redemption of my people is not yet, and I hereby declare and commit myself to be at one with them!" instead of giving him admiration and applause, those of whom I have been speaking would denounce him as an agent of American imperialism.

It is hard for me to understand and impossible for me to accept the perverted logic which provides sauce for the goose and not for the gander, the logic which makes it admirable to stand up for yourself and your own if you are a black and makes it contemptible if you are a Jew. I for one find nothing contemptible in it. I want to take this opportunity and every other opportunity—God grant me many!—to stand up and declare for myself, for my own, for my people.

There are a variety of patterns that have been developed in our society to cope with this kind of problem. Several of these are becoming more widespread, although in my opinion they not only do not succeed in dealing with the problem; they add to it. The first of these is, as an explicit ideology, rather old-fashioned, but as a matter of implicit attitude it is as fresh as the daily paper. The eighteenth century used to call it the ideal of "toleration"; in the nineteenth century, "toleration" became "tolerance"; in the twentieth century we know it as "apathy." We have come to a pretty pass when the most we hope for is that others will be indifferent to us.

I would like to be explicit about something about which explicitness has become almost a matter of embarrassment in recent times. Not very long ago, in response to continued, I won't say harassments, but depredations that cost human lives, Israel made a foray into the Beirut airport. She made very sure that human beings were cleared out, then set about destroying a number of planes. Not a single life was lost; no one so much as suffered a scratch. Yet the moral indignation around the world was unbelievable. Everyone expressed shock and horror at Israel's doing any such thing. But I do not recall that the Vatican expressed shock and horror at the blowing up of the Swiss airplane a few weeks ago. Those who profess to be deeply devoted to the highest human values do not recognize that things are happening in this world with regard to which we will not be silent again. Their silence remains deafening; at most, it is broken by a kind of sentimental rhetoric.

I spoke of the Vatican. Let me say that I am proud and grateful to be a graduate of the College of St. Thomas in St. Paul, Minnesota. Like millions of people throughout the world, I have a very warm and high regard for the late Pope John. A group of American Jews once visited Pope John, whose middle name was Joseph. He received them in audience; when they came in, he got off the papal throne, walked toward them, opened his arms, and said, "I am your brother Joseph." I do believe that he was, and I am happy to honor his memory. But there are many others, in all denominations, who could speak the same words and they would remain only words.

The great Hassidic Rabbi Simcha Bunam once said, "The distance between the heart and the mouth is as great as the distance between heaven and earth." But he added, "Yet the earth is nourished by rain from heaven." Words are not so bad, at least as a starting point; but it is getting to be hard to have even that, and when you do have it, questions still remain. I was not here in your city when the President of France was visiting you, but I read what reports of his visit I could get in the provincial press. I must say that it gave me scant comfort to hear his declaration that France is not an enemy of Israel or of the Jews; it is just that French policy requires that a certain amount of military equipment be made available to the enemies of Israel and the Jews! I was reminded of the great prayer of another Hassidic master, who once burst out on Yom Kippur, "Dear God, if you are not going to redeem your people, Israel, at least redeem the goyim!"

There is a second policy, which goes beyond toleration; that is emphasizing sameness instead of differences, and responding to others positively in terms of the samenesses. This is called the ecumenical movement. Or rather, it is miscalled that. A genuine ecumenism presupposes differences, which are recognized, accepted, and indeed appreciated. In this perspective, we relate to one another, not to deny or overcome differences, but so that in the light of the differences we can come to understand ourselves better and appreciate the other better. Genuine ecumenism has no more in common with what passes by that name than genuine equality between the sexes, and respect for one another, has in common with what is called "unisex," by which both sexes are degraded. What is fundamental here is the confusion that is becoming more and more widespread between community and identity, as though the only way to achieve community is to reduce each to the least common denominator.

I am an immigrant, of a family of immigrants; it has taken

a long time for me to come to the conclusion that there is something degrading about the notion of a melting pot. I do not want to be melted down. I do not believe that the greatness of America or of any other rich culture is the result of a process of decomposition of all the distinct cultural strains that enter into its make-up. I do not believe that what makes us great is to become like the ad man's description of milk, rich and creamy with homogenized goodness. We do not need homogenization. Whenever I hear people offer as an argument for simple human decency in the treatment of others that "After all, they're just like us," I tremble, waiting fearfully for the moment when it might be found out that I am *not* just like them. The man who appeals to the premise "They're just like us" is not capable of love; he can only see his own image reflected in the mirror. If he truly faces an *other*, all that is evoked in him is distrust, misunderstanding, and hostility.

There is a story I heard about the coronation of one of the last Viceroys of India, Lord Reading, Sir Rufus Isaacs. Picture what the coronation of the Viceroy of India might have been around the turn of the century, with the maharajahs resplendent in their robes and jewels. When a dignitary stepped forward and held out the Bible for Lord Reading to take his oath of office, he looked at it and said, "I cannot take my oath on this Bible; it is not mine." It included the New Testament as well as the Old. An aide was sent to find a Bible that consisted only of the Old Testament; there was none to be had. But it is not for nothing that the British have a reputation for great diplomatic skill. Someone stepped forward, took hold of the Bible, ripped out the New Testament, and gave Lord Reading the remainder, and he took his oath of office. There was not the least hint here of derogation of another faith; after all, most of those present were neither Jews nor Christians but Hindus and Moslems. It was only that Lord Reading was determined, as he should have been, to take his oath as the particular individual that he was, and not to permit himself to be absorbed into someone else's culture, whether British or Indian. He was his own man.

I had the inestimable privilege of being a student of the late Bertrand Russell. There is a story he told of something that happened to him at the time of the First World War, when he was jailed as a pacifist. When he was being admitted to the jail the bailiff was taking down his personal data and asked, "Religion?" Russell said defiantly, "Atheist." The bailiff said, "How's that?" "Atheist." And the bailiff said, "How do you spell that?" Russell spelled it out; the bailiff smiled gently and said, "Well, it doesn't matter, we all believe in the same God anyway."

I have heard that a television announcer last December was speaking about the commercialization of Christmas, and carried the same spirit so far as to say, "Let's put religion back into Christmas. This Christmas, go to the church or synagogue of your choice!" On that same irresistible theme, I must tell you also the apocryphal story of an American Undersecretary of State who, in the course of a recent debate at the U.N. on the Middle East crisis, was overheard to exclaim, "Why can't Israel and her Arab neighbors settle their differences like Christian gentlemen?" A Buddhist who overheard him said, "You know, the trouble is, I'm afraid, that that's just what they're doing!"

What I want to put in the place both of toleration and of so-called ecumenism is something very different—a pluralistic outlook in which we recognize, accept, and welcome differences. The essence of chauvinism, tribalism, or racism is to think that differences are not a matter of free choice for each person; indeed, to think that personality is not a free growth at all but something to be imposed from the outside. It is as monstrous to make of someone a Jew by what others do to him as it is to make of a Jew a Gentile by what others do to him, and the same is true for black, white, Hindu, Moslem, and every other human identification.

Underlying these monstrous ways of behaving toward one another is the notion that differences are always and everywhere relevant. I am confident that the women here would like to be recognized and appreciated as women; yet if you were applying for admission to a professional school, or you were a candidate for political office, or applying for an executive position, you would rightly feel it to be a monstrous injustice to be responded to as a woman in those contexts, where being female has nothing to do with your qualifications. Incidentally, there have recently been some fascinating court actions in this connection. Stewardesses, for instance, are arguing that the airlines have no justification for insisting that they not be married; being unmarried is not relevant to the performance of any duties that anybody is willing to be explicit about—that is not what the airlines are selling!

I have another example. The College of Cardinals is larger today than it has ever been, I believe. But not even the most sensitive and anxious Jew could complain of anti-Semitism because there is not a single Jew in the College of Cardinals!

That is one college where it is perfectly appropriate not to admit Jews. It is a very different matter if we consider, for instance, the proportion of Jews in college faculties in the United States, which is quite considerable, or the proportion of Jews among administrators of colleges in the United States, which is very, very small. Comparable, and in some ways more shocking statistics can be stated with regard to blacks and other disadvantaged groups, victims of injustice all over the world.

I believe it is important for all of us to repudiate, wherever we can, identifications imposed upon us from without which really have nothing to do with our identities. People talk about "Jewish" names, which are probably either German or Russian; they talk about "Jewish" faces, which are probably Mediterranean or Levantine; they talk about "Jewish" food, which most likely is Slavic or Central European; and so for a host of other superficial identifications, in themselves trivial, but not in their aggregate psychological and social effect.

Throughout our society there is tacitly accepted a kind of *axiom of linearity* with regard to values. This is the view that all values can be put on a single scale. They can all be lined up, so that if two of them occupy different points on the scale, one must be more valuable and the other less valuable. What I am proposing as a basis for human relationships is the negation of this axiom; it is this negation which constitutes genuine pluralism. Indeed, in the house of our Lord there are many mansions. When somebody reproached the Seer of Lublin for worshiping in his own way, he replied, "What kind of a God would it be who could be worshiped in only one way?" What is true of worship—that there must be as many ways of worship, when it is genuine, as there are worshipers—is also true of all other human aspirations.

Hawaii has some admirable features. But as one of the states of the United States it is not exempt from the problems I have been speaking of—though not with regard to Jews or blacks, who are an insignificant proportion of the population. Yet the fundamental problem of dealing with various racial and ethnic minorities is very much present there. The motto of the University of Hawaii is: "Above all races stands mankind."

I want to tell you one way in which they take this motto seriously. In itself I suppose it is not very important, but it provides an effective symbol. The University of Hawaii students elect a beauty queen, as many colleges do, but with this difference: they elect a dozen. I do not mean one queen and eleven princesses—runners-up, or second-class beauties. I mean they elect one who is Caucasian, one who is Hawaiian, one who is Japanese, one who is Filipino, one who is Chinese, one who is Korean, and so on. There is no reason under God's blue sky why all human beings must conform to some single standard of beauty. I believe that black is beautiful, just as is white, brown, red, yellow, and every other human color.

What is distressing is that, instead of cultivating the beauty each of us has as his own, we sometimes think we can achieve beauty by insisting on how ugly the other is, and worse, by taking others' lives in our hands and *making* them ugly. In this way we deny ourselves as much as them; there is no fulfillment either of their potentialities or of our own.

When I insist that there are many ways in which man can fulfill himself, I am also saying, in those great words of our tradition, *Hinei ma tov!* How beautiful it is for brothers to live together in unity! But there is a certain danger in constantly invoking the ideal of *loving* your neighbor. That may be a very high ideal, but I am afraid it is too high for most of us to take seriously these days. *I am not asking that my neighbor love me; I would only like to live in peace with him.* I would like to be able to live with him in the full measure of my humanity, without first agreeing that I will live, not *my* life, but his.

People say, "It is all very well for you Jews to insist on pluralism, on recognizing, accepting, and appreciating differences; but isn't it true that you yourselves accept a linear-value scale in which your people are superior to all others? How do you expect the rest of us to go along with that?" This argument is not just a matter of fanciful ideological debate; I have heard it in many discussions among young people struggling to know themselves and to accept themselves. For my part I believe that this is a serious misreading and distortion of our tradition, reinforced by just that mechanism I spoke of earlier of identifying with the aggressor. We have heard this charge from so many enemies that we have come to believe it ourselves. But it is not true. Jews differ from non-Jews, not in greater merit but in greater obligation. If anybody wants to assure me that I don't really have a greater obligation, I would be delighted and grateful. After the so-called Six-Day War, some wit in Israel swept the country with the proposal, "Now that we have recaptured Sinai, let's give back the Ten Commandments!"

Throughout our tradition, the difference between law and non-law which has always been emphasized has been solely in religious obligation. Apropos of the Ten Commandments, there is a useful, though not quite accurate, symbolism in the Two Tablets of the Law, one of which contains the religious obligations and the other the moral obligations. The last six of the Ten Commandments, making up the so-called Law of Noah, are universal in their application; Noah, after all, was a righteous man and not a Jew, since he lived before the time of the first Jew, Abraham. The general position of Judaism with regard to being "chosen" is that formulated memorably by the prophet Amos, who said, "To whom much is given, of him shall much be required."

This is a point of view which I have often had occasion to share with students in another connection, quite apart from Jewish identity. The proportion of the population, even of this richest country, which enjoys the privilege of a college education is only a few percent; on the world scene, those who have the opportunity for a college education are a fraction of one percent. I believe we owe a great deal in exchange for this privilege. We can discharge the obligation, not by always being docile and obedient, but by applying our knowledge and our skills to the betterment of our people, and indeed the betterment of all people. Today, Jews in Israel are fighting for their lives, and in other places for their identities. How monstrous to deny them help on the grounds that they claim to be better than others.

There is an extraordinary passage in the Midrash discussing the events immediately following the exodus from Egypt and the crossing of the Red Sea. When the Hebrews crossed to safety and freedom, they sang a song of rejoicing. At that moment, the Midrash relates, the angels were about to join in the song when God reproached them, saying, "My creatures are drowning; how do you presume to sing?" How remarkable that when a people is celebrating its triumph over its oppressors it can still hold forth the moral ideal of recognizing the common humanity which gives us reason to mourn even for the death of an enemy. That is a great ideal. I am proud to say that even in this time of crisis it seems to me that in the behavior of the Israelis such moral and human ideals are still present. May they always be present!

There is a final difficulty that presents itself. People imagine that the only morally sound basis for respect and acceptance of both self and other must be something universal and undifferentiated among all people. Whenever I speak of the values I find in a Jewish philosophy, or a Jewish identity, there are always those who protest, "But don't the Buddhists also say . . . ?" Or, "Isn't this also to be found in Hinduism?" And so on. In each case I have to reply, "Indeed, and perhaps even more than you are aware." Yet, what an extraordinary idea it is that only what is unique is valuable, as though the only basis on which I can appreciate and commit myself to the boundless values in my wife and my children is to take the position that no other woman and no other children have worth, or even matter to me. It seems to me that the psychological reality is exactly the contrary. Truly to appreciate one's own is to enhance the possibility of a sympathetic identification with the other, and truly to open oneself to the qualities of the other is to allow oneself to appreciate what one finds in oneself.

I would like to insist that pluralism is not just a device by means of which the Jew in a time of crisis hopes to win friends and influence people. Among the greatest documents of our history are not only national works like the Book of Esther, in which the hero, Mordecai, is introduced with the words, "There was a *Jew* who lived . . . ," but also universal works like the Book of Job, which begins, "There was a *man* who lived in Uz." Nowhere is there any mention that Job was Jew or Gentile, Moslem or Hindu, Christian or anything else; he was a man facing the universal problems of evil, of injustice, of coming to terms with his finitude in the face of his experiences of the divine.

This universalism has been an essential content of Judaism for millennia, but I believe it is not that which has to be emphasized today. Now I think a more strident note has to be sounded, but one which is nevertheless essential to the music. I believe we must now reaffirm the literal significance of that great question of Hillel's, "If I am not for myself, who will be?" The more closely I look at the situation of the Jew in America and the world, today and tomorrow and maybe the day after tomorrow, the more I feel that while there may be others who are for me, I am determined that first of all *I* will be for myself.

Ours is an age of contempt for the mind, an age of what Russell called "subjectivist madness," in which people suppose that all that counts is the content and quality of their own experience. It is an age in which some of the great values of civilization are being beclouded—the values of objectivity, of openness of mind, of rational discussion among intelligent men of good will to resolve differences. All these values, I

102

think, are more precarious today than they have been in my lifetime. I believe that here in the United States we are closer, God forbid, to a fascist regime than ever before. I am concerned about this, not only as a citizen, but also as the individual human being that I am. This means, among other things, as the Jew that I am. It is my faith that we Jews will not lend ourselves to the subjectivist madness, that we will not share in the contempt for the mind and its works, that we will not allow ourselves or any man to be degraded, that we will reject the illusion that we contribute to the dignity of any man by swallowing any man's contempt.

To do all this takes courage. That also I believe to be a great virtue of our people, and on this note I will close. It is traditional that when we conclude the annual reading of the whole Scripture, the Torah is held aloft and we recite in unison, *Hazak, hazak, v'nit'hazek!*—"Be strong, be strong, and let us strengthen one another!"

An Experiment in Openness

EDWARD FLANNERY

Secretariat for Catholic-Jewish Relations,
Bishops' Committee for Ecumenical
and Interreligious Affairs

The title of this discourse appears far removed from the theme of the present series. A preliminary word should be said about their connection. The theme, "Where are we? Where are we going?" can of course be applied to several perspectives. Does "we" represent our "one world"? The West? Or just the United States? Does it apply to our religious state or human life on the whole? I shall assume that the subject will gain in interest if its scope is narrowed to our own Western or American civilization, perhaps with an accent on the religious, which, if we are to believe some social historians, is the mother of culture.

The state of society in the West has until now depended to a large extent on the molding influence of ideas derived from Judaism and Christianity. It may be assumed again that to some extent this is still true. A case, of course, can equally be made for the decline of influence of these religions in contemporary society.

It may again be assumed that many of the critical problems of our time are reducible ultimately to this decline in the impact of Judaism and Christianity on the contemporary mind and society. The advent of the ecumenical era is based, I believe, largely on this assumption, and is an attempt to supply a remedy. Both religions are under the charge of irrelevancy, and not only from the side of the young. My question is: Can the decline and irrelevancy be attributed to some degree to the noncommunication of these two great religions, to the continuing estrangement that still separates them? It is my belief that such is the case. I believe, further, that the launching of the Jewish-Christian dialogue in our day is a recognition of this fact, and an attempt to do something about it.

My next point is that this dialogue itself has in its brief career fallen upon evil days, and since 1967 has languished. The churches were on that occasion accused of an immoral silence in face of another possible genocide. Jews generally have identified with Israel as a new dawn for world Jewry and Judaism. Christians in 1967 did not see it as such, but merely as a Middle Eastern state, of dubious validity, in trouble with its neighbors. The Six-Day War, thus, was a model of noncommunication between the Jewish and Christian communities. Since 1967 Israel has been made the center of the dialogue, and the touchstone of its survival and progress. For this reason, how Christians think about Israel is of great importance, and what Jews think they think about it is also.

The intent of the present discourse is to acquaint Jews with one Christian's attempt to educate his co-religionists about the State of Israel. It is an experiment in openness—an attempt of a Christian to speak to an imaginary Christian audience on Israel in front of Jews. The views expressed are not entirely representative of the Christian viewpoint, but contend to be such.

The Jewish-Christian dialogue has stumbled over the State of Israel. This fact was never more forcefully brought home to me than recently, when, asked what he expected of Christians today, an Orthodox rabbi replied: "Just respect our tie with the State of Israel, nothing else." It was plain that, for this rabbi, Israel epitomized his Judaism as well as the Jewish-Christian dialogue. His view is representative. There can no longer be any question but that the vast majority of Jews have identified with the State of Israel, whether they see it merely as a refuge from anti-Semitism, as a source of Jewish identity, or as a Messianic fulfillment. Israel has always been central to Jewish belief and to the Jewish soul, and in times of exile, an object of aspiration and prayer; the latest return to the Land has revived in Jews everywhere the sense of this centrality.

Jews are at present keenly disappointed by Christian attitudes toward Israel. They are aware that most Christians form a spectrum that veers from cold neutrality to a not so cold hostility toward that state. They note, too, the new neutrality of the United States and feel that they must go it alone. Now that ghettoization of Jews in Western society has come to an end, they find their land of promise ghettoized among the nations.

Their disappointment in Christians results from a feeling of having been let down. In the wake of two millennia of oppression at Christian hands, the Vatican Council renounced the "deicide charge," rejected anti-Semitism, underscored the special bond between Judaism and the Church, and called for "fraternal dialogues" between Christians and Jews. Though somewhat incredulous, Jews took these directives seriously, hopefully seeing them as a promise of a new day for Jewish-Christian relations. The Six-Day War in 1967 became the test of the promise and the "Christian silence" that accompanied it became its repudiation. Some Jews (and Christians) say the Jewish-Christian dialogue died during the war; all observers admit it broke down and has languished ever since.

The aim of this discourse is to explore, in the light of this breakdown of the dialogue, Christian attitudes toward the State of Israel, ostensibly the chief source of the breakdown. The view presented is not, of course, the only possible view of the matter, but it is, I hold, more consonant with Christian attitudes than its competitors. There are many views of Israel among Christians, but some of them must be considered non-Christian, others again indeed quite un-Christian. There are those who believe, for example, that they must adopt an anti-Israeli stance if only to placate Arab wrath. Then there are those who claim to be merely "anti-Zionist," for one reason or another. Others will discuss the State of Israel only in terms of Arab refugees. And finally, there are those who obviously speak of Israel with clear overtones of anti-Semitism, more or less disguised or admitted. Views inspired solely by motives of American national self-interest are not considered here; they must be considered more chauvinist than Christian. National self-interest can be a legitimate norm but certainly not the ultimate one for a Christian.

A certain dilemma affects anyone who enters this area of discussion. So controverted are the issues involved and so high-pitched the emotions attaching to them that one can say nothing favorable to one side of the conflict without appearing to offend the other. Loyalty to the truth will overcome this dilemma. There is, of course, that "evenhandedness" which tries to practice perfect equality, praising or criticizing both sides with precise parity, but at the cost of satisfying no one and saying nothing. Such evenhandedness will be avoided here.

My method is a simple one. Discussion will center on certain basic issues around which most misinformation and myths have accumulated, such as Zionism, the legal validity of the State of Israel, refugees, and the significance, theological or other, of the State of Israel. The discussion aims to be succinct, even lapidary, which means that no attempt at full proof of propositions will be given. For this, repair must be had to the standard studies. My main objective will be to supply certain important facts, truths, and emphases that are frequently omitted in the discussion of the conflict in the Middle East. These omissions have seriously impaired the dialogue.

108

Preliminary to the question of Israel is that of Zionism—a major source of myths, misinformation, and confusion. It is *de rigeur* among critics of Israel to make a hard-and-fast distinction between Zionism and Judaism or, for that matter, between Zionism and Jewry. Briefly, the argument usually runs: the State of Israel is not a product of Judaism but of Zionism. Judaism is a religion; Zionism, a modern political movement. Moreover, all Jews are not Zionists.

Judaism is in reality essentially Zionist. From its inception it was conceived as a sort of trinity: a people, a Torah, and a land. To a considerable degree these concepts were considered interchangeable, as the old Jewish adage indicates: "The land, the people, and the Torah are one." The Hebrew Scriptures, the Talmud, Jewish literature, medieval and modern, and the Jewish liturgy are in truth replete with the idea of possession of Zion (which represented the whole land) and return to it after every exile. In this context modern political Zionism, launched by Theodor Herzl, must be seen as a latter-day political manifestation of the Messianic core of Judaism itself. The nineteenth-century attempt to de-Zionize Judaism attempted by Reform Judaism, in appreciation for emancipation, and present similar efforts have not succeeded. Today the overwhelming majority of Jews are Zionist or pro-Zionist. No one can contradict this without appealing to exceptions or to mavericks in the Jewish community. It is particularly indelicate of Christians, it seems to me, to attempt to seek out Jewish anti-Zionists in order to bolster criticism of Israel or espouse Arab interests.

One can understand Jewish dismay and chagrin at a certain conception of Zionism so often found not only in Arab propaganda but also on the lips of Christian critics of Israel. What to Jews is a word of honor and a sacred tradition is portrayed as a sinister conspiracy or aggression. From Soviet spokesmen, Arab apologists, and Christian critics one hears of "official" Zionism, "imperialist" Zionism, "world" Zionism, and the like, subtle efforts to dissociate Zionism from Judaism, or from the Jewish people as such, thereby opening the way to unrestrained attack on the Israeli state.

Where this calumnious notion of Zionism comes from should be clear. Certainly not from historical study. There has never been anything covert or sinister about Zionism, as the least acquaintance with its history will show (or as a reading of Rabbi Arthur Hertzberg's *The Zionist Idea* and Ben Halpern's *The Idea of the Jewish State* likewise will). From the start the movement split into two groups, one which wanted, with Herzl, to seek a charter for the Jewish state from all governments concerned; and a second, which placed the accent on settlement in Palestine by purchase and cultivation of land—with Arab cooperation.

There are two quite different views of Zionism. One is contained in its official records beginning with the First International Zionist Congress in Basel in 1897. The other is contained in the *Protocols of the Learned Elders of Zion*, which has been rightly named the "greatest forgery in history." In the latter, Zionism appears as a dangerous and cryptic conspiracy vowed to world conquest. The *Proto-*

cols were quickly proven spurious but nevertheless enjoyed a vast readership long thereafter. They were widely circulated in the United States a few decades ago. They circulate still in Egypt today and are also published in the United States by anti-Semitic houses. It is impossible not to detect traces of the *Protocols* in the weird caricature of Zionism one encounters so often in present discussions of the Middle East conflict.

The attempt to dissociate Zionism and Judaism is doomed to failure. Each has always been an integral part of the other, and this is as true today as ever. Unless Christians understand and accept this centrality of the land in the Jewish self-conception, true dialogue with Jews becomes impossible. The charge that "injecting" the State of Israel into the dialogue is illicit because it is "political" will not do. Zionism has religious and ecumenical roots. Those who, because of troubles in the Middle East today, wish to bar Zionism from the dialogue are the ones who really inject politics into a truly religious and ecumenical matter. The usual charge of politics must thus be reversed.

The question may be asked whether Christian anti-Zionists are conversant with the existence and history of Christian Zionism. It is an interesting and instructive but little-known page in our history. It should be reread today. It would show that Christian pro-Zionism is not necessarily merely a response to Jewish insistence but an impulse that may find its energy in Christianity itself. It is an interesting fact that some of the British inspirers and architects of the Balfour Declaration, which began the political development of the Jewish state, were motivated in part by Christian Zionism. Another root of that state was anti-Semitism in Christian countries. Thus, ironically, have Christians indirectly had a double hand, one negative, one positive, in the creation of the State of Israel.

II. FOUNDATIONS OF THE STATE OF ISRAEL

The root-issue in the Arab-Israeli conflict is Israel's right to exist in peace and security. It is the denial of this right by Israel's enemies that has, for the greatest part, produced during the last twenty-three years three wars, the Arab refugee problem, and the present explosive situation in the Middle East. The effective resolution of this issue could, moreover, all but solve other issues and problems involved in the situation; failure to resolve it renders their solution all but impossible.

And yet about this crucial issue circulates more misinformation, vagueness, and wishful thinking than around any other relating to the conflict. The aim of this paper is to examine, much too briefly, the foundations of the State of Israel and to remedy some of the usual lacunae affecting its discussion. I am aware of the controversy raging around the subject. The discussion of it appears often to take the form of a kind of "intellectual terrorism." It would indeed be difficult to find an issue more in need of rational dialogue. Perhaps because of the bitterness separating Arabs and Jews today, it is the role of Western Christians to initiate this dialogue.

Historically, this discussion does not go beyond 1949, when Israel was accepted as a member of the United Nations.

The vicissitudes of the problem that followed that date have no decisive bearing on the question of Israel's basic right to exist as a state. It is a significant fact that most arguments against this right are frequently drawn from happenings after 1949—proof again of the confusion on the issue.

While my intent is strongly to affirm Israel's claim to a secure existence, I am not insensitive to the rights and aspirations of the Palestinian Arabs. They too have rights, and a right to a state of their own. This latter right, however, cannot be made into a right to have what comprises the Israeli state within secure and negotiated boundaries. Arab rights and grievances require a treatment separate from that of Israel's right to its own state.

Some say that Israel must be accepted as a brute fact, that the history of the last twenty-three years simply cannot be undone. This, to my mind, is not adequate justification for the State of Israel. If this is to rest on firm ground, its foundation must be proved legal and moral. It is my thesis that the Israeli state is thus firmly founded, as firmly, both juridically and morally, as any other state in the world, indeed better founded than many. There would of course be no just grounds to impose on Israel standards and requirements of existence not asked of other states.

Many Christians, sometimes encouraged by Jewish spokesmen, believe that Israel's claim to the land is based on an original possession of it in Biblical times. It is a false basis. This Biblical possession can of course provide Israel with theological significance but can provide no legitimate political foundation today. This manner of legitimating the state forms a *non sequitur* that should not be used by Jew or

Christian. Today a political conclusion cannot be drawn from theological or scriptural premises.

To concede Israel a valid foundation, juridical and moral norms binding in the present are necessary. Only on such a basis can the common canard that the Jews stole the land from its rightful owners, the Arabs, be put to rest.

Did they steal it? The answer to this question broaches the juridical aspect of the problem. Of course they did not, as anyone familiar with the history of the Zionist movement knows. The ingress of Jews to Palestine and the acquisition of a juridical basis for a Jewish state comprise a record of overt settlement by peaceful purchase and by political strategy going back at least to the last quarter of the nineteenth century. The crescendo of violence that marked the latter part of that period came from Arab opposition to these businesslike and legal efforts. In no sense was it the result of Jewish appropriation or aggression.

It is not my intent to describe the colonizing or political developments that brought the State of Israel into being. Any reasonably unbiased history of the period will give the necessary details. A few comments, meanwhile, will suffice for this purpose.

Much playing with figures and statistics by Israel's opponents goes on. By a selectivity of both figures and dates it is made to appear that Jews formed a minuscule part of the population of Palestine at any selected time. *The essential fact is that in that part of Palestine assigned to Israel in 1948 by the United Nations Jews made up a majority.* This majority had come into being under Turkish and British rule, so in no sense, I repeat, could it have been the result of

114

conquest or aggression. (The smuggling in of Jews during the Hitlerian genocide did not add substantially to the general total.)

The ingress of Jews into Palestine occurred under international encouragement from 1917 on, with the issuance of the Balfour Declaration. (This encouragement, true, diminished after 1939 with the appearance of a British White Paper that year—at a moment when Jews were in greatest need of immigration to Israel in flight from Hitler.) Much opprobrium is heaped on the Balfour Declaration by anti-Israelis, while much stock is placed in the Sykes-Picot agreement, a secret treaty of 1916, a McMahon letter to Sherif Hussein the year before (later repudiated), and the like. The fact is that these latter never were accorded any real political efficacy and soon fell into desuetude, whereas the Balfour principle was incorporated into all major political instruments touching the Middle East, including the peace treaties of San Remo and Sèvres of 1920, the Palestine Mandate of 1922, the Churchill White Paper of the same year, and, in an attenuated form, even the White Paper of 1939.

Despite growing Arab opposition to the Balfour principle and the prospect of a Jewish state, these survived and finally culminated in 1947 in a vote of the General Assembly of the United Nations (33 to 13, with 10 abstentions) to partition Palestine (excluding of course Trans-Jordan) between the Jewish and Arab populations. In a rare show of agreement, the United States and Russia voted together for the partition. As the Jewish state was set up, five Arab armies marched against it. This first of the Arab-Israeli wars, initiated by Arabs, altered the partition boundaries and originated the refugee problem. What was to have been the Palestinian Arab State was annexed by Jordan in 1950.

In 1949 Israel was accepted as a member of the United Nations. Two attempts were made thereafter by the Arab bloc in that body to place the establishment of Israel before the World Court. Each attempt was voted down, which proves at least that the United Nations did not consider that it had acted hastily or unwisely.

The argument that an action may be legal yet immoral is often leveled by Arab opinion against the U.N.'s establishment of the State of Israel. The argument should be taken seriously. If Palestine was wholly an Arab land, even the mere 8,000 square miles finally allotted to Israel would be a questionable development. Was Palestine an Arab land?

Two determinations must be made before answering this question: In what sense, and at what period, was it Arab?

Certainly it was never Arab by any national claim; Palestinian Arab nationalism is of recent origin. As an outpost on the edge of empires to the north, east, and south throughout the centuries, it was never claimed as a geopolitic entity— except by the Crusaders, who occupied it as the site of the holy places. In more recent times it became a province in the Ottoman Empire, until it was mandated to Britain after World War I. In the last thirteen centuries, in sum, it has changed hands fourteen times and never attained independence of any kind until 1948, when it was partitioned into separate Arab and Jewish states. Politically, then, Palestine was never an Arab state or nation.

As to population, the Arab claim is stronger, for although

116

Palestine was never without its Jewish and non-Arab population, Arabs formed a decided, if fluctuating, majority in Palestine as a whole. Several times in Christian times, on the other hand, it was the cultural and spiritual center of world Jewry. Jersualem has had a Jewish majority for many years.

These considerations, of course, raise the question of popular self-determination. But it must be remembered this principle is a recent one, not fully accepted until after World War I. Even in the days of the Balfour Declaration and the Sykes-Picot secret treaty, lands and states were allotted by victorious colonial powers, not by popular suffrage. The Balfour principle, which finally obtained, promised, moreover, that the rights of Arabs as well as Jews would be respected. The United Nations, when it partitioned Palestine in 1947, respected the population composition. As already pointed out, the Israeli portion contained a Jewish majority—and this was before the Arab refugees had departed. The Arabs were allotted portions wherein they were the majority.

To speak then of "Palestine" as an "Arab land" is misleading, if not false. The partitioning of it into two states (or three, counting Trans-Jordan) was a politically necessary, judicially adequate, and morally just action. Criticisms can be made of the actions and policies of the Zionists and later the Israelis, and more again of those of the colonial powers, especially Britain, but these criticisms cannot be made into an argument against the validity of the State of Israel as such. Arab peoples and interests have been injured over the years, but these wrongs have come as much from Britain,

117

Arab countries, and Palestinian Arab policies as from the Zionists or Israelis. The last are usually blamed for all, however.

If there is ever to be peace in the Middle East, if there is ever to be a dialogue between both sides of the conflict there, Israel's valid right to exist as a state must be clarified—and accepted. Any solution that denies it, it should be clear, is one that will obtain only at the price of perpetual war that will lead to the destruction of both sides. Those who talk of "binationalism" or an "Arab Palestine" at this date in history should own up to this fact. Some of course may say that even perpetual war is acceptable if justice is served. Anti-Israel opinion sometimes argues in this direction. They must be reminded that to destroy the State of Israel would be one of the gravest injustices as well as an unspeakable carnage.

III. ARAB REFUGEES

To many viewers of the Arab-Israeli conflict, the Arab refugee problem stands as the paramount issue. They regard all other aspects of the conflict through its optic. Unfortunately, the optic is a distorting one, for it tends to blind the beholder to other issues and dimensions of the problem that are also of greatest importance, such as, for example, Israel's survival, Jewish refugees, Arab-Israeli or world peace, and the like. If our approach to the refugee problem is not to remain purely sentimental, its relation to these and other problems must be considered. To do so is in no sense to downgrade the refugee problem.

It is important at the outset to emphasize the human aspect of the refugees' plight. Obviously, it is a tragic one that must invite the sympathy and concern of the very least of humanitarians, let alone of Christians. This concern and sympathy, however, must be genuine, more genuine than that of those who shed copious tears for Arab refugees but have not as much as a kind word for other cases of hardship in the conflict, especially Jewish, and who never fail to turn their concern for the Arab refugees into a cudgel with which to beat Israel. As much as any Arab government, these sympathizers use the refugees as political pawns and thus place their tears under suspicion. If we, as Christians, are to utter the truth in love, moreover, mere sentiment is not enough, and the truth as exact as we can make it is also a requirement. It is a requirement not found in every Christian account of the tragedy.

The aim of the discussion is to attempt to place the problem in a truer perspective, not by outlining the multiple facts of this highly complex issue, but merely by remedying some of the omissions and scotching some of the myths with which the propaganda of both sides of the conflict has clouded the problem.

The refugee problem is a derivative of Arab-Israeli wars, and these at their deepest root are in turn products of the Arab refusal to accept the right of Israel to exist in security and peace. It is true that the departure of many of the refugees predated the Arab invasion of Israel in 1948, but even this merely anticipated the oncoming war. Arab spokesmen had made it clear in 1947 that they would oppose by force the establishment of Israel.

119

Much dispute has centered on the cause of the exodus. Jews claim the refugees left merely to get clear of the area of conflict and that they were largely encouraged by their leaders to do so, with the understanding that they would return upon Israel's destruction. Arabs claim that they were forced or frightened out by Israelis as a matter of policy. It will perhaps never be fully determined what proportions of truth must be allotted to these explanations. The picture is no doubt a mixed one. The best likelihood is that the majority left to escape the dangers of the battlefield. Many others did not want to live under Israeli rule. Some, especially in the Haifa area, were encouraged by Arabs to leave. And no doubt some left for fear of Israeli vengeance. In some cases the fear was real; in others, imagined. It would seem, to sum up, that the large majority left of their own accord.

Why the refugees were not allowed to return is a question that must be answered in political terms. For Israelis, their repatriation, compensation, and resettlement became a price of recognition of their state and cessation of belligerency. For Arabs, from the beginning, repatriation became the necessary condition of any talks and eventually an undisguised device to weaken or destroy the Israeli state whether from within or from without. Israelis cannot forget Nasser's observation of September 1, 1960: "If the refugees return to Israel, Israel will cease to exist." Thus were the refugees used politically by both sides.

Another subtle manner in which they are used politically is evinced by that type of discussion of the problem which tends to insinuate that the refugees, some 1.5 or 2 million strong (inflated figures), languish on the borders of Israel watching the farms and properties from which they were expelled by 2 million (a minimized figure) predatory Israelis who have appropriated their country. In this way is Israel made to appear to belong wholly to the refugees; the Israelis to appear as thieving interlopers. By innuendo the refugees thus become a political argument against the very right of the State of Israel to exist. The innuendo is usually reinforced by heart-rending stories of pauperized refugees pointing pathetically to their former homes, farms, or properties in the State of Israel, now in Jewish hands. Much hatred of Israel among non-Arab Christians has been aroused in this way. Unbiased estimates indicate that no more than 10 percent of those refugees who once lived in Israel would opt for repatriation. It may be added here that six years ago the U.N. Commissioner General of the United Nations Relief and Works Agency for Palestine Refugees reported that 50 to 60 percent of registered refugees were either economically independent or partially self-supporting.

A word must be said about the number of refugees. Divergences here again are considerable. It is a tendency of anti-Zionists to exaggerate the total. Scholarly studies tend to find even U.N.R.W.A.'s figure high and place the original refugees in 1948 as between 500,000 and 600,000, not 800,000 or 900,000, and the present number of veritable refugees at about 1,300,000, not 1.5 or 2 million. It is important to distinguish, as is seldom done, between refugees who actually lived in Israel proper and those who did not. Exact figures still await exact censuses. Until 1967, Arab refugees and Arab governments refused to allow exact censuses, with

121

the result that considerable trafficking in ration cards has gone on.

Israelis, rightfully, bring up the consideration of their own refugees. They estimate that some 600,000 or 700,000 Jews were forced out of Arab lands without compensation, and tend to see these as a legitimate exchange of refugees. The obvious difference, of course, is that Israel has completely absorbed its refugees, while Arab countries either could not or would not absorb theirs. Rarely is reference to Jewish refugees made in Christian accounts.

The complaint is often heard that Israel has refused to do anything about the Arab refugee problem—a false accusation. It is true that as time went on and refugee camps became more and more centers of hostility and of terrorist recruitment against Israel, Israel refused more and more to consider repatriation as a solution, holding rather for repatriation of separated family members and of a token number of the remainder on condition that they return in peace, and for compensation and resettlement of the rest. Israel has, nevertheless, made overtures from the start to negotiate the problem, but has always been rebuffed. As late as 1967, Israel proposed to negotiate a five-year plan for the rehabilitation of the refugees prior to general peace negotiations, thus making an exception to her general policy—but to no avail. The same offer has been made twice since, again to no avail. Meanwhile, Israel has contributed considerably to their welfare: in 1968 contributing $2,500,000 to U.N.R.W.A., to which $1,000,000 for various needs and services must be added. At least these amounts will be spent in the present fiscal year. During 1968–69, 16,374 permits to refugees to return were issued, but over 7,000 were not used. These return permits have been offered for use again since. Since the Six-Day War, unemployment has disappeared in the Gaza Strip and has greatly decreased on the West Bank, where jobs are conceded indiscriminately. Many plans have been proposed to solve the problem in the Knesset, and the government is presently experimenting with model farms as a pilot project. These efforts often run against Arab opposition and so have to be disguised so as not to appear as cooperation with Israel.

There can be little question but that, practically, the refugee problem is the chief obstacle to peace in the Middle East; indeed, the most immediate source of war. There is little question but that more could and should be done by Israel, by Arab countries, and the United Nations to solve it. If the deadlock is to be broken, generous gestures are necessary on all sides. All sides must, meanwhile, cease to use the problem for political ends. In this country any sympathy for the refugees that harbors a hatred of Zionism or Israel, if not of Jews, should be forsworn—and unmasked. Any solution that does not entail love and understanding for all concerned in the tragedy or that tends to promote hatred of either side can be considered neither a Christian nor a moral one.

IV. SOME THEOLOGICAL CONSIDERATIONS

One might expect that a Christian could not look upon the State of Israel without certain scriptural and theological reverberations. The people of the Bible back in the land of the Bible is a development that should remind him, however vaguely, of his origins. But often this is not the case. Many Christians see Israel as a purely political and secular affair and refuse to see any possible connection between it and the Israel of old.

The purpose of this part is to investigate this refusal and also the possibility of conferring a theological significance on the latest return of Jews to Israel. Nothing will be stated in a didactic spirit but rather as an effort to pose questions that Christian as well as Jewish theologians should face. There is a "positive theology" that is expected to revise its conclusions in the light of happenings in the world that may conceal theological implications. These have been called "signs of the times." Israel is one of them.

A primary consideration which seems to inhibit many, including theologians, is a fear that theological or scriptural considerations may be used to serve as a political validation of the Israeli state. These fears are vain. Our earlier discussion has tried to show that the State of Israel can be firmly founded without the least religious reference. The politics of the State of Israel and its theology should be kept scrupulously apart. On the other hand, political beliefs hostile to the State of Israel cannot, in their turn, be allowed to inhibit an open and honest theological exploration of Israel's existence and meaning.

The alleged lack of resemblance between the present State of Israel and the old Israel of Biblical times is frequently argued by anti-Zionists. These critics, seeing Israel in a myopic light, fail to see the genuinely religious character that marks even Israel's secular endeavors. Israel reminds us that the religious is not synonymous with the cultic. Any visitor to a kibbutz will understand this. It is interesting, on the other hand, that when Israel is not being accused of secularism it is usually described as a theocracy, a religious establishment, much as it was in its earliest days. There has, in any case, always been only one Israel, whether it worshiped its One God or at the altars of Baal. Moreover, is not expecting a beleaguered state not yet a quarter of a century old to fulfill its highest ideals demanding something expected of no other country?

The question may be asked: Is not the refusal to allow a theological consideration of Israel a residue of the deicidal myth, which often included the idea that Israel could never return to its homeland or Temple, or again of that old theology of rejection which consigned Israel to obsoleteness in the Christian dispensation? Possibly. Certainly the deicide charge is no longer tenable for a Catholic. But can it not stay on as a kind of unconscious hangover and take the form of a vague uneasiness at the prospect of the Holy Land, particularly Jerusalem, in the hands of the Jews? The widespread anti-Zionism among Christians, at all events, can hardly be accounted for by the rationale of their arguments, so often lacking in substance. It would be wise for us to suspect that some of the old anti-Judaic attitudes and feelings of the past are still operative, at least unconsciously.

It is not possible to undertake a theological study of the State of Israel without the benefit of a thorough renewal of the traditional Christian theology of Judaism, which as yet is hardly begun. More than a refutation of the deicide charge is required. The Vatican II declaration (*Nostra Aetate*, 4) has already opened the way by signalizing the spiritual bond that unites church and synagogue and by summarizing some pertinent parts of St. Paul's Epistle to the Romans. Writing about thirty years within the Christian dispensation, the Apostle makes clear that Jews still "have the covenants . . . and the promises. . . ." (Rom. 9:4–5); that "God's gifts are irrevocable" (Rom. 11:29); that, because of our common patrimony, Jews are "most dear" (Rom. 11:28). No further proof should be needed of Judaism's continuing election and its special status in the Christian outlook, its special claim on Christian affection. We have here an essential part of the authentic Christian attitude toward Jews and Judaism, which, unhappily, disappeared in the course of the centuries in favor of the deicide and rejection theories.

An acknowledgment of Israel's ongoing election in the plan of God invites a review of other presuppositions of the old anti-Judaism. This latter rested on a variety of assumptions which grew up in that bitter period when church and synagogue separated all too harshly. In the main, these assumptions saw Judaism (1) as *nothing but* a preparation for the Gospel; (2) as something that should disappear with the advent of Christ; (3) as a faith that was, at least at the time of Christ, decadent, legalistic, and perverse; (4) and, after Christ, as an obsolete faith without spiritual substance; and (5) as fated to live on only as "witnesses to the truth of the Church and to their own iniquity" (St. Augustine).

Recent historical, scriptural, and theological investigation has found all these estimates to be in one degree or another wrong. From them has flowed, however, what may well be called a semi-Marcionism, which draws its inspiration from

126

that second-century heretic Marcion who rejected the Old Testament as the word of a Demiurge rather than God. Though condemned by the Church, Marcionism has not ceased to tempt Christians and no doubt has found some veiled expression in the tendency that would completely de-Judaize the Church, reduce the Old Testament to a mere handbook of pious reflections, and allegorize it practically out of existence. All of which has ostensibly led to a weakening of Biblical faith and of the belief that God may still write large in history as in days of old.

If it can be said that the Christian theology of Judaism is far from fully renewed, it can be said that a Christian theology of Israel as a land does not exist. And doubtless it will not exist until the former is well under way. Its creation, further, will probably not make much headway in the present atmosphere, so inflamed by the Arab-Israeli conflict, one side of which would, it seems, bar the merest consideration that Israel might have a religious significance. Be that as it may, if we are not entirely to politicize theology, certain questions regarding Israel must be posed to the theologians even now.

Can the return of Jews to Israel in our time have a scriptural or theological meaning for a Christian? We will not receive much help here from Jews, who themselves are not completely sure about it. Anyhow, this is a matter of Biblical faith, which certainly is not—or should not be—the exclusive prerogative of the Jew. Though the Christian may seek help from the Jewish believer, he is here on his own.

In his *Israel: Echo of Eternity*, Rabbi Abraham Heschel challenges Christian theologians to reconsider their age-old habit of allegorizing everything in the Old Testament while literalizing all in the New. And, indeed, in response the Christian can question whether *everything* in the Old Testament was fulfilled in Christ. There are, clearly, things in the Old Covenant that not only were not fulfilled but were unfulfillable. Christ did not propose to fulfill all Messianic expectations of the Old Covenant; rather did He ignore some, and even contradicted others. Could not some of such expectations still hold out for fulfillment in later times, particularly those which appear to pertain to eschatological times? Cannot some of them have to do with the post-Biblical interim that is the present? If not, why not? Moreover, in the light of the Epistle to the Romans (9–11), the fulfillment of the Old Covenant in Christ cannot be understood to entail its disappearance.

Further, if we must believe with St. Paul that Judaism still has the covenants and promises (Rom. 9:4–5), and these originally involved the land, on what ground is the land excluded from them in post-Biblical times? The ancient prophecies always spoke of a divine pattern or sequence, involving sin, exile from the land, repentance, and return to the land. Whereupon, would Israel's latest exile elude these prophecies?

Such are some of the questions that seek answers from the theologian. The Christian theology of Judaism of the past will render him little help, and the present situation in the Middle East will act as a deterrent. Hence, his research will probably be a prolonged one. In the meantime, judgment on the theological implications of present-day Israel must be cautious, tentative. It is perhaps time for the Christian, in face of the State of Israel, to reciprocate Rabbi Gamaliel's tolerance of the primitive Church: "If this plan or work is of men, it will be overthrown; but if it is of God, you will not be able to overthrow it. Else perhaps you may find yourselves fighting even against God" (Acts 5:38–9).

The Living God
and the
Dying Religious Style

EUGENE B. BOROWITZ

Professor of Theology,
Hebrew Union College-Jewish
Institute of Religion, New York

Theology implies eternal ideas and perennial principles. How appealing that sounds amidst the change and confusion of our world. How nice it would be if reflection about faith could anchor us in the immutable and render us secure.

Theology has done anything but that in recent years. The movement of religious ideas has been so rapid that when I first received the invitation to participate in this lecture series about the future, I thought I would have to speak about "the Death of God." To me, that intellectual position seemed already moribund, but I attributed my diagnosis of its dismal condition to my subjectivity and made a mental note to face up to what others still took seriously. As it turns out, I was too tender-minded. That theological fashion is as dead as Nehru jackets. Even its successor movement, the secularization of religious thought, is well on the wane—except for those Roman Catholics who are discovering that one cannot usefully build the city of God in segregation from the city of man. Currently the theological swingers are big on celebration. With ratiocination demanding and politics bloody, they prefer to revel in the religiosity of play. Why should stroboscopic lights and lurid colors, the delights of the senses and the immanent aesthetics of the body, belong to the young alone? So professional thinkers have become quite serious about joy. Perhaps religion is dead but the academic study of religion has never been livelier.

Since we expect the permanent from theology, these rapid swings in fashionable religious thinking have given many people great anxiety. Believers cannot locate the old faith. Skeptics are convinced religion has entered on its death throes. Imagine: priests threaten to picket the Pope; Protestant seminarians strike to study sociology rather than New Testament Greek; Jewish radicals praise the Al Fatah. Perhaps the Death of God movement faded so quickly because of its success. Perhaps God is dead.

I do not doubt that for a great many people that is true. They live their lives without Him, fully occupied trying to stay sane, even useful, in a hectic time. For such people the Death of God movement had nothing new to say and they rightly ignored it. What created the sensation was that, instead of being an attack by outsiders, the new atheism arose from within the ranks of the believing and announced the need of a new way of being faithful. The future of religion, we were told, rests on our ability to appropriate the truth that God is dead—a thesis which one can most charitably describe as mistaken. There is a great risk in making radical statements, as recent events have made clear. When one says daring things so as to force the wishy-washy to take a stand, they are as likely to line up against you as with you. Compared to our grandfathers, it is clear we think of ourselves as unbelievers. We are hardly so dogmatic as to declare ourselves atheists. Rather we prefer to think of ourselves as open but unconvinced. There is hardly a more intellectually self-satisfying position in the modern world, in any field, than genteel, worldly agnosticism. The Death of God movement, however, radicalized many a person out of that old smugness. We came to realize that while we didn't believe very much, we also didn't believe quite that little.

That became most clear through the question of human values; that is, personal ethics and social welfare. The turmoil and tumult in our civilization, the new stridency and the old repressiveness, have made us realize how precious some things are to us, how important it is for men to be good to one another, and how vital it is that society become just and compassionate. Humaneness is more than a utilitarian arrangement or a pragmatic contrivance. It is a matter of ultimate significance, of cosmic meaning. We have discovered we care that deeply about man and mankind.

But if God is dead, all things are permitted. We could not help but be sympathetic to the cry: If there is an Auschwitz, there cannot be a God. But what shall we say to its logical consequence: Since there is no God, Auschwitz is natural, or permitted? That goes too far. Any theory which allows for, which vindicates, such utter evil cannot be tolerated.

132

We may not have much certainty about God, but we know we cannot abandon man. If there is anything we are certain about, it is that our lives and our society are given us to perfect. In accepting that task of perfection and working at it as best we can, we find the meaning of existence. We cannot learn that truth from within ourselves, for we are the problem. We cannot gain it from society, for that is what requires correction. Modern science is value-free, and contemporary philosophy no longer teaches why men should do anything. It takes novelists as diverse as Saul Bellow and Norman Mailer to remind us of what is stirring deep within ourselves, that we believe more than we will admit, that, in fact, we live more by faith than by brain, that, in truth, we still stand covenanted to a God we do not understand.

God is alive and hiding in the midst of us.

That alone explains what the reporters have thus far not remarked upon. The intellectual and personal interest in religious thought these days is unprecedented. Some time ago one might have believed that was due to the daring of the Death of God movement. But from Zen Buddhism to Sokko Gakkai, from the *I Ching* to Meister Eckhart, the new waves of thought and the new styles of religious expression continue to evoke extraordinary concern. Not a decade ago, theology was recondite and mysticism shameful. Today they are news. If religious publishers are in difficulty, it is because the religious market has broken out of the clerical ghetto into the real world. Talk about meaning and duty and life-style is not the prerogative of the professionally pious. It is the everyday concern of post-affluent, post-pleasure, post-agnostic searchers. One need not look far for experimentation with liturgy, with living in community, with taking a stand to expose and defeat evil.

To me the conclusion is obvious: the tribulations of religion arise not because modern man is irreligious but, on the contrary, because he feels contemporary religion is not religious enough. Nowhere is that more visible than in the priests and nuns who have left the Roman Catholic Church. Mostly they have not had a sudden loss of faith. Rather, out of love of God, devotion to the Christ, commitment to the Christian community, they have had to seek a new life. They are as devout as ever. The only faith they lost was in their organization. To remain faithful, they broke with their institution. The same is true of many of the protesters and experimenters in Protestantism and Judaism. They devise liturgical happenings because the old forms do not bring them close enough to God or do not do so intensely enough. They live together in communes or eat together in community so that the love they know is God's chief command may transfigure the style of their daily association. On issues where we mutter or manage to write a check, they take their unpopular stand so as not to lose their immortal souls. The numbers of these religious explorers is minuscule. But they are not thereby insignificant. They put the lie to the assertion that modern man cannot be religious and will not live by faith and its disciplines. They say rather that insipid religion, leisure-time religion, occasional religion, is the pervading heresy of our time. They take Paul Tillich seriously. Only an *ultimate* concern is worth calling God. Any commitment of lesser involvement, no matter how sacerdotal its style, no matter how ecclesiastical its language, is idolatry.

God remains the supreme ironist. We thought the challenge was that we had to defend Him against those who said we must get rid of Him. Now He has raised up against us a generation of rebellious existentialists who insist we have betrayed just what it was we thought we had been so nobly defending.

God is not dead and religion is not dying, if we mean by that, man's living relationship with Him. Rather, it is in God's name that the new attack has been mounted against church and synagogue. If they are His servants, why do they not show Him forth better? If they are our means to communion with Him, why do they create so many barriers between us and Him? The questions cannot be diverted with calls for proper respect and better manners. The men who ask them speak too authentically from the values we ourselves affirm for us merely to be kind where we are called upon to be responsive. Though it may pain us to admit our institutions are not models of contemporary righteousness, much less saintliness, we should remember that before the High Priest might make atonement for the sanctuary or the people of Israel on the Day of Atonement, he was required, every year, first to ask God's pardon for himself and his family.

Let us begin with the most radical position; namely, that religion is best practiced without any institutions whatsoever. That notion arises not only from our continual disappointment with religious functionaries and at religious functions but from the nineteenth-century philosophy that religion is primarily a subjective affair. No man whose sense of faith is rooted in the Bible need dispute that proposition, for, to cite the most obvious case, the Book of Psalms establishes it beyond doubt. But the religious anarchists are arguing more than that the individual is necessary. They insist that the individual is a sufficient category of religiosity. Individualism is especially appealing today because we are systematically robbed of our individuality by the technological apparatus of our society. And for Jews, its appeal is irresistible—for if all men were considered as individuals, no Jew would ever be reminded of his traditional obligations or be invested with the disabilities of minority status.

There are many virtues in the contemporary reassertion of individualism. Yet the insistence that society and institutions have no significant role in the life of man must be rejected. Two separate lines of argument blend together here. The first builds from within. Man needs structures to help him overcome his evil urge. Considering what we have seen men do in our time, it is difficult to accept the hippie thesis that if men were only natural with one another, society would have no problems. Of course we would prefer to think of ourselves as innocents and our world as the Garden of Eden, but it is our sinfulness which powers history. Woodstock may have been a beautiful human experience. But it lasted only a weekend and it left so much debris scattered over the countryside that what was gained in fellowship was almost lost in pollution. We do not defeat the evil urge in us by denying it is there. Rather, that is the beginning of its ultimate triumph. Our best hope in the reality of history is to acknowledge our capacity to damage, to struggle against it, and to find the social structures which can aid us in that never-ending fight.

136

It is the peculiar genius of an institution—and thus, inevitably, its curse as well—that it transcends the individual. Sometimes a man may dominate it, or a given personality may shape it in terms of his gifts. But if it is a good institution, it outlives its founder and carries on its function with lesser men guiding it. Thus, synagogues survive their rabbis and their officers; schools, their faculties; art museums and symphony orchestras, their directors. And that is true of the constituents as well. Members may come and go, even a group may depart, but as long as the institution is alive, it has a character which transcends the given individual who participates in it. That is why it may hope to guide and judge him, to strengthen him in his weakness and provide a channel for his power. So in religion, the institution mirrors God's relationship to man. For just as God has a status and a permanence and an authority beyond any individual's, so does the institution which seeks to embody His will on earth. Thus, when a religious institution is true to its Lord, it serves as a unique means of helping man find a proper relationship with God. More, left to ourselves, we become easy marks for the evil urge. We learn, not only to betray God, but to be satisfied with ourselves despite it. We say we do not need institutions to be religious, but rarely do we turn out private saints.

Institutions are not people-proof. They often have been perverted by men's evil urges. Yet, despite their frequent failings, religious institutions have the hope of transcending not only us but also themselves. That is because they admit that they exist to serve God. They remember and keep current the old words about Him, they preserve the testimonies of prophets and saints concerning Him, and they acknowledge that they too stand under His judgment. Of all human institutions, it is remarkable how over the centuries the church/synagogue has been able to generate its own cleansing. Is there a more remarkable instance of devotion to the idea of institutional self-correction than the Jewish law which mandates a weekly reading from the prophets, specifically ones which contain the most violent criticism of religious institutions and the religious community?

There is a second need for religious institutions and it too stems from their transcendent character. They are needed to fulfill the individual's responsibility to society. On this matter, religious sensibilities differ. For some people and, in a way, for some religions, it is enough for the individual to save himself. That is an appealing option today. Society has become so unmanageable, even other people are so difficult to help, that it seems a sufficient accomplishment to build a satisfactory life for ourselves. No wonder people are tempted to try one of the meditative Eastern faiths or, more privately and technologically, marijuana.

Judaism is distinguished among the religions of mankind by its central concern with society and history. Its Bible is neither a book of spirtual or mystical formulae nor a series of philosophic disquisitions, rationally analyzing the absolute. It is mainly a book of history and law which considers it almost self-evident that it is not good for man to dwell alone, and takes it for granted that the fate of any individual cannot be separated from the destiny of all mankind. It does not know hermits and it does not counsel withdrawal. It will not compromise man's social responsibility or free him from a role in the redemption of all mankind. No wonder we have difficulty accepting its teaching.

Religious institutions exist so that the individual may have his proper effect on human destiny. They amplify his power through time and space, and keep it effective until the Messiah comes. They are not a substitute for the state or the market or the place where neighbors meet. Those centers of the interchange of power have their legitimate place in a world where religion is taken seriously, but we may not count on any of them to transform man and perfect society. The religious institution is founded just for that. We may not be in the mood to serve our brothers, having been so idealistic yesterday, but our institution will not forget. We may have despaired of the power of righteousness because we have accomplished so little, but our church or synagogue, though it may falter, will carry on and refuse to surrender. Religious institutions perpetuate courage and eternalize hope.

This amplification of the individual's responsibility is particularly important because corporate evil regularly tends to outstrip personal evil. We are vicious enough in what we do to those we know to warrant a major transformation of self. We are far worse when involved with social instrumentalities. Because they transcend us, we feel ourselves less implicated in the sins we commit against them or through them. So we regularly do things in our cities and our corporations and our clubs that personally we would consider utterly impermissible. With institutions so strong and the individual so weak, there must, at least, be one voice of equivalent strength speaking for man. There must be one power in society which has the capacity of standing up to all the other powers in judgment and for instruction. To be sure, religious institutions can themselves do more damage in God's name than any single religionist would do on his own. If we feel betrayed by them, it is because we do not want them to be merely human and ordinarily sinful. We want them to be more Godlike than anything else man creates, and when they are as petty and deceitful as any other human body, we lose faith not only in them but also in their God. That is to ask too much of them, that they be only godly and not human as well. It is such an extraordinary thing among the exploitative powers and oppressive principalities of this world that any institution should faithfully speak for God much of the time that we should cherish its sporadic authenticity. For, on the corporate level, until the Kingdom of God comes on earth, it is the most authentic voice we will regularly hear.

That intense social concern of Biblical religion has received new support and much invigoration from the recent shift of intellectual interest from individual to social concern. Two decades ago, in the heyday of psychologism and the popular discovery of psychiatry, we believed we could attain peace of mind by coming to terms with our emotions. Our claims today would be far less grandiose but no less significant. We can all list a dozen or so people we know who would obviously benefit from psychiatric treatment. But what good does it do to be well adjusted to an exploitative social order? In that frame of reference, psychology becomes the new opiate of the masses. We want to give the underprivileged mental-health clinics when what they need is jobs and housing and education and a social structure committed to their welfare. Today it is sociology which excites hope and arouses imagination. Instead of describing the abstract patterns of social behavior, sociologists have turned to charting the means by which we oppress one another. They have made us realize that the social order is a human creation, that there is no divine right of deprivation and degradation. What we have made, we can remake. What has for so long simply gone its own way can now be made to work for the betterment of all men. That is an ancient Biblical concern, now given new statement and power. It confirms the need for religious institutions but makes clearer than ever their social responsibility.

The trauma of religion in our time then is neither God nor institutionality. Because we believe in the one, we must utilize the other. Our agony with them is, and I repeat that it is a religious agony, that they do their work so poorly. If religious institutions are designed to help us serve God on both a personal and a social level then the simple truth is that we find them too impersonal to us as individuals and too insensitive to the moral ills of our society.

I am not talking only about congregational life but about every sort of religious institution. Let me clarify what I mean by illustrating the way in which these criticisms apply to our theological seminaries. Where classes are big, students complain that they are not known as persons. Where classes are small, the objection is raised that curricula do not permit them to study what, even within the classic sources, they genuinely wish to learn. Where the faculty is reasonably competent academically and pedagogically, students resent the fact that there are no saints in residence, no models for them personally to follow. And then they are aghast that this school of religion seems only another competitive academy rather than a genuine community of brothers; they are disgusted that this embodiment of their faith centers so much on its existence and its scholarly goals that it has no energy or interest for the society outside its walls.

These demands are impossible of fulfillment as they stand. They are also right. Perhaps I am partial to them because I share the existentialist analysis, which engenders them, of what it means to be a whole person. In any case, I do not think our seminaries will have a significant future if they do not begin to try to meet them. Our learning cannot remain so impersonal and antisocial if we are long to take religious study seriously.

A more devastating judgment is being made everywhere concerning the local synagogue or church. For the moment let us forget about the organizations, the hierarchies, commissions, and councils. Let us speak of what we know best, the single congregation. What regularly disturbs us there is not its insistence that God is alive or its desire to serve Him but the self-defeating manner in which it goes about it. The problem is not an archaic content but an obsolete style. Our local congregations follow a royal mode of conduct when we live in a democratic world. They are God-centered in so false a way that they leave almost no room for man. It is as if we are not certain enough that we believe in Him to be on more equal terms with Him. So our institutions are primarily concerned with dignity and impressiveness when we want to escape the impersonality of society and simply be ourselves. They are most authoritative about etiquette, which in every other area of society we have unmasked as falsifying and ir-

142

relevant. They think being solemn and ponderous will prove how devoted we are when really all we want is a little hope and a little inspiration. This style no longer enables worshipers to serve God. Rather, it demands we serve its proprieties, and that is why it leaves us outraged.

Let me give three specific examples of what I mean—rhetoric, music, and architecture—each of them as related to the personal function of institutions. Clergymen are almost instantly recognizable by their peculiar diction. If they serve the college-educated, their language regularly tends to be abstract, elliptic, and polysyllabic. Only ambassadors speak with equal pomposity—and they, we know, are employed to use the best of words to hide the worst of consciences. To be sure, the modern minister or rabbi is not as repulsive to the ear as he was some years ago, when one had the impression that he thought his pulpit was an extension of the Roman Forum or the House of Commons. Nonetheless, the accepted style reeks of the superior speaking to the inferior. It is so beyond response and argument that it leaves little place for us, the listeners, as active, thoughtful, engaged human beings. We are not beyond listening respectfully to other people, provided they have genuine respect for us. If the clergy wish to speak as God's representatives, then they must find a way to address us which in tone and manner indicates that they know we too are created in His image and share in His covenant.

Our congregational music is also impersonal. We think it is at its best when it is done by competent professionals. The result is that, instead of praying through the music, we listen to the beauty. As so often in our society, we are reduced to being spectators. If anything, we are made to feel impotent before our God, for we are obviously inept by the standards of such competence. What a shame it is that the organ has become the chief instrument of our religious music-making. It is distinguished from all other single instruments for its ability to produce huge, engulfing waves of sound. Its effectiveness comes from being housed in rooms gigantic enough to accommodate its enormous tones, and it is because of the vastness of the space that, when quiet, it makes such an impression. In any case, the great organs do not encourage us to express ourselves. They overwhelm us with their sound. They engulf us in grandeur. But they thereby depersonalize us. We are not fiefs groveling before our liege lord, but covenant partners renewing our relationship. We could not be other than respectful, but we wish to be respected as well.

And the same may be said of the huge sanctuary. Its legitimacy arises from its testimony to the majesty of God. That is important to sense in our society—but surely not at the price of once again being awed into feeling that in the face of the greatness of things we are nothing. Often the sanctuaries are so large they work to separate us from our brothers in the congregation. We cannot see them. Perhaps we cannot even hear them. We came seeking community and the very building has once again fragmented our existence.

This royal mode dominates the style of all our religious activities. It came into being to give due glory to God, and for those to whom that is the essence of religion, the older style will remain attractive. But for most of us today the justification of religious institutions is not primarily what they do for God but what they do for man. Our surprising search for God, our need for God, our longed-for relation with God is more for our sake than for His. It must affirm us as much as glorify Him. It must upbuild us as much as it exalts Him. Nowhere else in our society do we have access to the transcendent reality which gives us an ultimate dignity that is inalienable. To be denied that unique sense of who and what we are by the manner of our religious activities is to remove from us the one thing religion alone might have furnished us.

I forbear from saying much about the failure of religious institutions on the social/ethical level. The case is overly obvious. Religious institutions should be leading our society in sensitivity to the occurrence of evil, in concern for the remedying of evil, in judgment of our apathy toward evil. Rather, our institutions, where they have not positively refused to become involved in the issues that affected men's lives, have regularly lagged behind sensitive spirits in the nation, often secularly inspired. But this, too, relates to the older religious style. Adopting the royal mode meant taking the king and his court seriously. It bred the desire to associate with them, to be accepted by them, to be commended by them. It made respectability the chief religious goal. For people who still feel that way, it is the height of religious accomplishment that President Nixon has Sunday-morning services in the White House. For others, that very pride betrays a false sense of value. The power structure does not assign religion its worth. Rather, God the King of Kings calls every man of power into judgment and stands over against every nation with His plumb line of righteousness.

Our religious style need not be impolite to show itself authentic or rowdy to show itself genuine. But neither can we be satisfied to call the monarchist conventions of the older religious fashion an adequate means for modern man to find himself in serving God. A generation that has applied the tests of personal authenticity and social concern to home and school and nation will rightly insist that they be best exemplified in religious institutions.

I see no good reason to resist these demands for change. The only religious institution divinely ordained was the Temple in Jerusalem. It was destroyed not once but twice. It has never been rebuilt, and most traditional opinion says that only the Messiah could do so. Since then, many other institutions have arisen among the Jews, most notably the synagogue and the school. Having known such inner revolution, how can we insist on the irreformability of our present religious style? God did not ordain it and He does not require it. What He requires of us and what we, because of Him, require of our institutions today is that we, through them, become true human beings, and, through us, our society become a true community.

Building New Foundations

ELLIS RIVKIN

Professor of History,
Hebrew Union College-Jewish
Institute of Religion, Cincinnati

We are going through one of the great watersheds in history and we are very uncertain as to where we are headed. There are no road maps and no certain and secure routings. Everything seems all at once to be disintegrating: our cities, our interpersonal relationships, our value systems. Standards are collapsing everywhere. No one knows any longer what is true, good, or beautiful. The sturdy supports of learning and knowledge, the colleges and the universities, are seemingly rooted in quicksand. Morality and ethics are being auctioned off daily to the loudest and most defiant bidder. Religion is exposed as the word of the Establishment; it is no longer the word of God. Wisdom is sought from the tousled, the long-haired, and the prematurely bearded, not from the hoary-headed and the graybeard. Vintage knowledge has soured, while freshly pressed doctrines intoxicate and exhilarate. The ego ideal has become Mao, not Moses; Uncle Ho, not Uncle Sam; Che Guevara and not George Washington, or Thomas Jefferson, or Abraham Lincoln, or for that matter, even Franklin D. Roosevelt or John F. Kennedy. A child today no longer dreams of growing up to be President but of overthrowing the Establishment. The Bible and the Gospels are valued for their glimpses into social struggles of yesteryear, for their anticipation of the thoughts of Marx, Lenin, Marcuse, and Mao, rather than as a treasure trove of how sinful man can make peace with himself and with his God.

We are, I am convinced, witnessing the disintegration and collapse of a world built on scarcity and the emergence of a world built on abundance. We are undergoing the agony of the transition from a world of rivalrous and warring nation-states to a collaborative global community; from a world of colonialism, imperialism, and clientism to a world of developmentalism; from a world of constraint to a world of freedom. But far more is being born in the pain, suffering, and despair of our day. We are on the threshold of the *Age of Humanity*. Man's long and seemingly hopeless struggle to elevate himself beyond his prehuman and subhuman limitations—his entrapment in the need to exploit and kill his fellow-man so that *he* might live, an entrapment from which there was no escape so long as scarce resources could not sustain abundant life—is now on the verge of achievement. Is there any wonder then that the earth shakes and violence abounds and the heart and mind of man quiver with awe and fear?

148

What gives me such confidence, when what we actually are experiencing is so dreadful and so seemingly without hope? "Patterns from the past" is my rejoinder. The world as experienced by contemporaries, especially in the great periods of transition and during the great watersheds of history, was never a reliable indicator of where the world was going. In every such age, the participants failed to discern from what *seemed to be* the direction, what indeed it *proved to be*. They fastened their attention on the immediacy of their experience, the clear call of their senses, the prevailing assumptions of their minds. They rarely, if ever, looked beneath the surface to determine whether there might not be powerful long-range forces fashioning out of the stuff of the present a future that did not seem likely or possible. In retrospect, we know that non-Christian contemporaries of Jesus did not anticipate the triumph of Christianity in the Roman world; the medieval Church had no inkling that Luther would spin off a massive revolution against its magisterium; proud Venice did not read the signs of its inexorable decline; nor did the English of Victoria's day foresee the setting of the sun on their far-flung empire, or the piping out of their fleets from the strategic seas and oceans.

This discrepancy between phenomenal surmise and actual outcome has proved, throughout history, to be a constant. In retrospect, historians and political scientists have discovered again and again that that which *seemed to be* most potent and causal *proved to be* transient and ephemeral. Contrariwise, those factors which were either overlooked entirely or were brushed aside as irrelevant turned out to be the forces that directed and shaped the future. Perhaps this point should be illustrated by an example or two. A few years ago a remarkable study was published by a German historian, Georg Fischer, entitled, *Germany's Aims in the First World War* (New York, 1967). His archival researches exposed, for the first time, an array of secret data revealing not only that the Chancellor Bethmann-Hollweg had sought to precipitate the war but also that the war aims of Germany contemplated a continental and imperial system under German hegemony. These aims were modified only to the degree that their fulfillment became an impossibility; i.e., to the degree that German coercive power was insufficient to achieve these objectives. What is noteworthy about Fischer's study is that (1) it confirms an entrapment hypothesis (namely, that German capitalism had to find a way to expand beyond its territorial borders or face collapse); (2) it reveals that decisive policies making for war or peace were known only to a handful of individuals who made up the ruling elite; and (3) it documents the deliberate falsification of the record to conceal the manipulation and the aims of the decision-makers. What is most striking about Fischer's archival findings is that they were effectively kept hidden from the prying eyes of a generation of scholars who, following World War II, scoured the archives under the impression that all that was vital had been opened to their scrutiny. The most significant outcome of their researches was the notion that Germany was largely innocent of the guilt that the Allies had attributed to her; i.e., a lower level of documentation communicated the opposite of a higher. Neither the German people nor the peoples that were to be arrayed for and against her had any awareness of what was activating the decision-makers.

Let me now cite another example of more recent vintage. Former Secretary of State Dean Acheson in his recently published *Present at the Creation* shares with us the concern that agitated the decision-makers of the United States in the late forties. Disturbed over the growing evidence of Soviet expansion into Europe and fearful of the consequences for the West if the United States did not undertake the building of a powerful military establishment, these responsible leaders prepared a document approved by the National Security Council which, according to Acheson, bears the label NSC Memo No. 68. This Memo, according to Acheson, laid down basic principles that were to be determinative for United States policy: the massive build-up to constrain, blunt, and roll back the Soviet advance. This Memo was not circulated to the press and was not communicated in toto beyond the restricted membership of the National Security Council. The first inklings that such a Memo even existed were not forthcoming until 1967. And, to be especially noted, Acheson, writing two decades after its original formulation, informs us that this Memo still may not be quoted directly and only some of its general principles may be paraphrased.

The issue here is not whether secrecy is justified—I for one have no illusions about the need for restricting data-sharing in an imperfect world divided among contending sovereign powers armed with awesome weapons—but that what was *not* known was far more decisive than what was. Truman, Acheson, and those ultimately responsible for the security of the nation acted in reference to knowledge that they had but the public at large did not. And this commitment to secrecy transcends political party; for the legislation setting up the Central Intelligence Agency and the National Security Council was not partisan legislation. Yet it established *by law* institutions for covert operations and intelligence-gathering and processing which are prohibited *by law* from communicating to unauthorized individuals, irrespective of their rank, either their operations or their knowledge. And lest anyone deprecate the methods that have been devised for ensuring secrecy, let him ask himself what he knew about the U-2 flights *before* the Powers incident; or what he knew about the funding of leftist student and labor groups by the C.I.A. *before* the decision to phase out such operations; or what he knows *now* about the text of NSC Memo No. 68.

Clearly then, the surface of events and the flow of words are not likely to be helpful in assessing long-run trends. Since the past looks radically different to a historian than it did to contemporaries, and since, in our own contemporaneous world, we have legally established institutions committed to noncommunication, would not a historian looking for signs and omens of the world to come be best advised to look to those long-range forces which, though unseen, may be shaping both the present and the future and which—unlike the jumble of discrete events that blur and confuse, and the patter of rhetoric that diverts the mind—cannot be either concealed or denied? They have in the past proved to be far more determinative. In a word, what one must do is to view the present as though it were past, to view today as though it were already yesterday, and tomorrow as though it were today. From such a vantage point, one would grant the historian the right to separate the enduring from the transient, and permit him to indulge in the notion that subterranean forces are far more decisive than the superficial.

What then are these forces that might throw light on our present condition and justify the prediction that we are living through the travail attending the birth of humanity and not the pain of a terminal disease? For my part, I would single out one that I would regard as ultimately decisive: the patterns of capitalistic development since the sixteenth century.

Capitalism is the most powerful single force that has shaped the Western world and that has pressured the mind into fashioning the ideational responses of bewildering variety that have been both the shame and the glory of Western civilization. If we simply follow the vicissitudes of capitalistic development, we can make intelligible not only the seemingly confused and inchoate past but much of the bewildering and agonizing present as well. This will also reveal the grounds for my confidence that we are, despite signs to the contrary, on the threshold of the *Age of Humanity*.

I will state my thesis as simply as possible. Capitalism is a process, not an entity. It is a name appropriately applied to a multi-phasic developmental system, driven by the profit motive, that emerged in the sixteenth century. It has continuously transformed itself through the centuries and has become in our own day a vast complex of corporate structures. Its most distinctive feature is its built-in bias for change and development, a bias that is grounded in the profit motive itself; i.e., there is the lure of windfall profits for innovators. This inner dynamic precludes a serene and repetitive history. The pursuit of profit simultaneously dismantles and innovates. The more efficient forms of capitalism are always undermining the less efficient. Consequently, the preeminent form of capitalism in one epoch becomes a vestigial form in the next. The history of capitalism is strewn with the wreckage of its changing forms: mercantile capitalism yielded to laissez-faire industrialism, laissez-faire industrialism of thousands of individual manufacturers gave way to the corporation; the corporation organized to produce a single end-product generated the diversified corporation; the last, in turn, laid the groundwork for the conglomerate and the multinational and transnational corporation. All these forms are capitalistic forms, sequentially interrelated by virtue of an essential principle: the pursuit of profit. The principle of capitalism is thus separable from and transcends its forms. Capitalism is whatever the pursuit of profit makes it; or, to phrase it somewhat differently, capitalism is whatever capitalists in the pursuit of profit make it. Its definition is a historical, not a categorical definition and in that sense it is continuously open to redefinition.

The pressure of capitalistic development generated radical thinking because capitalism radically transformed interpersonal relationships. Radical thought, however far removed it might be from economic concerns, was a challenge to the traditional modes of thinking upholding pre-capitalist economic, social, and political structures. It was the means whereby people's thinking could undergo the kind of alteration which would impel them to reject ideas for which they had formerly had an intellectual and emotional attachment and to substitute for them ideas highly novel and alien. But since thinking involves symbolic forms, the alterations proceeded in a manner appropriate to the autonomy of ideas and symbols; i.e., they began with ideas, notions, beliefs already present which served as seeding points and language salients for innovation and novelty. Thus a Biblical verse, saturated with divine authority, could be drawn upon to yield a justification and a rationale for taking up arms in England against the Established Church and a sinning king. Once, however, the process of reassessment was let loose, it took on a momentum of its own, ending up with a batch of ideas and notions that had not been anticipated, such as the grounding by John Locke of state sovereignty in natural and inalienable rights.

Radical thinking since the sixteenth century has shown itself to be the ideational instrumentality for refashioning minds, even as capitalistic development was the instrumentality for restructuring society and its institutions. Or perhaps it would be more meaningful to say that since radical thinking always presupposes a prior alteration in the economic structure, capitalism, as a system committed by its inner dynamic to the dissolution of precapitalistic structures and of its own less efficient and obsolescing forms, is compelled to underpin radical and innovative ideational and symbolic systems *so long as it is developmental.* Capitalism can forgo radicalism only when it stagnates and disintegrates; i.e., when its dynamic principle of self-renovation and innovation fails to function. Radicalism, in turn, expires when there is no longer any provocation from economic change and development. That radical thought is not self-sustaining but rests on a developing capitalistic foundation has been proved by its extinction in the Soviet Union and in Maoist China. Once radicalism in these countries had been successfully utilized as an instrument for destroying the old order, it was canonized into a verbal system for sustaining the noncapitalist political elite and for periodically destroying recalcitrant minds. *Developing* capitalism is the only system thus far that has both generated and sustained innovating ideational systems, even when these have exposed capitalism as exploitative, callous, materialistic, crass, and utterly inhumane. The only free markets for *all* brands of Marxism and radicalism are to be found in capitalistic countries.

The radicalizing consequences of capitalist development went hand in hand with the process of its spread throughout Europe. Since it spun off revolutionary upheavals wherever it gained a secure beachhead, it was resisted by the old order. The precapitalist regimes were not ready to give up their power, their institutions, and their ideational and symbolic realms without bitter and bloody resistance. This resistance could no more be limited to brute economic claims and counter-claims than the capitalistic revolution could overthrow the old order without transforming minds and hearts. The struggle then between capitalism and precapitalism was as much a struggle for minds as it was for bodies. But because the ideational and symbolic realms are not economic and are not limited by economic laws, the content of ideas and the mental images evoked had about them a transcendental quality. They possessed a freedom uncurbed by concrete limitations; a freedom that was limited only by the creative capacity of the mind, the range of possible linguistic combinations, the degree of adaptability of language to new coinage, and the total ideational stock stored in the memory and locked in the emotions. An individual might thus be so stirred by an idea, a dream, a vision, as to give his life for its fulfillment, only to suffer disillusionment when its potency was blunted by economic, social, and political limitations.

The spread of capitalism—an economic form—spawned ideational systems—noneconomic mental images, states, and ideas—which proved to be refractory for securing a world restructured for the pursuit of profit. In the eighteenth century, the appeal to Reason proved to be very effective in exposing the precapitalist world as a travesty of Nature's design. The old order was dismissed as an affront to intelligence and a caricature of man's noble destiny. Life, Liberty and the Pursuit of Happiness rivaled Liberty, Equality and Fraternity as the catchcry of Reason, exciting minds and energizing hearts to topple divinely sanctioned kings and God-ordained churches. The end result was the American and French Revolutions and the arming of Napoleon with an array of ideational weapons which could blast away the mental and spiritual defenses of the old regimes.

But these ideational weapons were not as ideal as Napoleon had imagined. The old regimes, frightened by the prospect of sharing the fate of their regal peer, Louis XVI, rallied behind them the active support and enthusiasm of their subjects by appealing, not to the God of Reason, but to the God of their fathers, to the God of the old regime, to the God who had placed his imprimatur upon variation, differentiation, even upon unreason itself. In a word, the struggle against Napoleon unleashed Romanticism and elevated nationalism to the throne of glory. Reason as the instrumentality for capitalist development was blunted. Entrepreneurialism was more and more compelled to abandon its universalistic drive and to make peace with the nation-state.

This affirmation needs clarification. Capitalism is an economic system geared to the pursuit of profit. It consequently recognizes no territorial or ideational limits. Entrepreneurs seek out the most profitable areas for widening or deepening the market, for increasing the productivity of labor and capital, for integrating and exploiting technological innovation. An entrepreneur as such is not a religious, national, or racial category. Whether he be Jew, Protestant, Catholic, or atheist; whether he be English, French, German, American, or Japanese, he shares the same drives and is measured by the same impersonal standard of relative efficiency; i.e., his ability to make profit in a framework of competition. Capitalism may therefore be defined as an economic system that transcends religion, nationality, race, *and* ideology; it is an economic form with a built-in bias for a global framework supportive of its driving principle. The first great entrepreneurs, it will be recalled, made their great fortunes exploiting the high profitability of the ocean routes to the Far East. Ideally then, if entrepreneurs had been free to shape the world as best suited their interests and if they had been free to fashion whatever ideational system they pleased, they would have opted for a global community and a set of universal principles committing the mind to life, liberty, and the pursuit of profit. This bias for the universal was indeed translated by the Glorious Revolution in England, and by the American and French Revolutions, into such principles as life, liberty, property, pursuit of happiness, equality, fraternity—all seeking to impress upon the mind of man that these were inalienable and designed by Nature and Nature's God. The inalienable quality was vouchsafed by Nature and not religion, nation, race, or class.

The process of translating capitalistic development into these universal principles was disrupted by the defeat of Napoleon and the triumph of Romanticism. In retrospect, Napoleon had made a valiant and almost successful effort at opening up the entire European continent for capitalistic development. By dismantling and destroying at one fell swoop all the old regimes of Europe, he was in effect demolishing the stubborn obstacles to unimpeded capitalistic development and creating the foundations for a European common market; i.e., he was seeking to accomplish for Europe what the United States did indeed accomplish in America: the subordination of nation-state sovereignty to integrative sovereignty—the joining together of difference for the attainment of constructive long-range ends rather than the aggravating of difference for the attainment of limited and short-term ends. Had Napoleon been successful, Europe might have been spared the destructive nation-state wars which came very close to destroying both capitalism and Western civilization.

But he was not successful. He was defeated by the power still residing in precapitalist systems, a power as yet insufficiently corroded by capitalistic development in Central and Eastern Europe. The old regimes were able to marshal the mind-shapers behind them, and these shapers created a rationale that was appealing to deeply rooted psychic predispositions in man; there was so much truth in Romanticism that it had a transcendental appeal, lifting it high above such crass concerns as economic systems and the austere, emotion-stripped, and impersonal categories of universal Reason. To die on the battlefield for one's fatherland, for one's family, for one's soil was far more appealing than dying for an abstraction. Indeed, to galvanize his own armies and to draw from them the last full measure, Napoleon himself stoked the fires of nationalism.

But the power of precapitalistic societies in and of itself may not have proved sufficient to blunt Napoleon's drive. The *coup de grâce* was administered by the most developed capitalist state in Europe at the time, England. By throwing her support to the old regimes, she tipped the balance in favor of a fragmented Europe and doomed the Continent to nation-statism; i.e., the primacy of nation-state sovereignty over integrative-federal sovereignty.

From the theoretical viewpoint being advanced here, the decision of England sacrificed the universal dynamic of capitalism to the particular interests of entrepreneurs who happened to be operating out of England and not France. Instead of looking to Napoleon as the instrument for widening the sphere of capitalist enterprise, they looked upon him as a threat to their immediate interests. Instead of allying themselves with him to make the world safe for capitalistic development, they joined up with the old regimes to keep France in check. Instead of embracing the integrative-federal principle developing in the United States, England opted for the limited nation-state principle of enclosing within a limited framework of territorial sovereignty an economic system that must either expand or die.

But why did the most advanced capitalist society in Europe opt for what, in retrospect, was a disastrous choice? The answer is simple. Capitalism is a universal economic system, but it developed historically. The territorial state had emerged in Europe prior to the birth of entrepreneurialism. It had been fashioned out of feudal concepts and institutions. Its shape was largely determined by dynastic rivalries, not rational economic goals. Little, if any, thought was given to the optimal mode of organizing an area in the interests of rational economic integration. When, therefore, capitalism emerged, it emerged within the legal contours and institutional framework of the territorial state. For entrepreneurs, the initial concern was not with restructuring the world but with restructuring the territorial segment which served as their home base. The Dutch entrepreneurs thus carved out Holland, not because they rejected the southern Netherlands but because this was all they could hold and defend. The same held true for the English and the French. The entrepreneurs in each of these territorial segments had enough problems creating a national enclave without being saddled with the burden of a capitalist manifest destiny for the world. Once enclosed within the nation-state framework, the entrepreneurs sought to utilize the state to further their interests against those of their rivals enclosed in other territorial nation-state enclaves. Thus the competitive principle, which was translated into the law of the capitalist nation-state as a principle that *must* not be drawn upon to justify the physi-

161

cal destruction of competitors. Competitive claims between states again and again were resolved by the very violence which was prohibited within the state. The only limitation to such interstate violence was the power of another state to counteract with equivalent or greater power. This then was the paradox of capitalism as a historically evolving economic system: though universal, it was fragmented into distinct nation-state enclaves; though geared by a principle spurring and sustaining competition, it justified violence against nation-state rivals to gain competitive advantage; though driven to undercut, dismantle, and restructure precapitalist systems, it was used now by this state, now by that, to shore them up. When England cast its lot with Prussia, Austria, and Russia against Napoleon, it not only betrayed the capitalist principle that had made the nation so strong and wealthy, but also opened the sluice gates for that rampant nationalism that was to justify claims to coercive national sovereignty over every plot of European ground around whose sacred soil some hallowed memory, some linguistic variation, some unshared custom, some elusive wisp of special feeling could be garlanded, and for the preservation of which even the first fruits of the womb were not deemed too demanding a sacrifice.

In this sense, capitalism, as an economic system transcending the nation-state and other man-made obstacles to its dynamic global thrust, met its defeat with Napoleon at Waterloo. Europe, far from being integrated by developing capitalism, was fragmented by it. Within each territorial area, capitalistic penetration and consolidation was followed by an onslaught against the old regime and its institutions, but the results were a haphazard congerie of irrationally bounded nation-states. Entrepreneurs settled for what they could get, not for what was optimal.

This is dramatically illustrated by Bismarck's unification of Germany. Austria was left out because Bismarck recognized the limits of his coercive power, even though her territories were essential from the point of view of economic rationality. The Hapsburgs were not primarily seen as obstacles to the capitalistic revolution but as sovereigns to be courted as allies to blunt the power of other sovereign nation-states. The Austro-Hungarian Empire thus became a seething cauldron of dissatisfied nationalities determined to sever themselves from Hapsburg domination but with little other than intense nationalism to sustain a viable nation. The disintegrating Empire did not serve as the clarion call for *integrating* nationalities, territories, and resources, but rather for rallying around the fragmenting shards. Whereas in Western Europe the rise of capitalism had been followed by the drawing together of diverse autonomies into a unity of difference—even diversity of language proved no insuperable obstacle in Switzerland—the penetration of capitalism into Central Europe, the Balkans, and Eastern Europe undermined the unity symbolized by the Hapsburg, Ottoman, and Romanoff dynasties by underwriting every diversity that could conjure up national enthusiasm. Each of these nationalisms, unsecured by economic viability, became free-floating valences available for combinations with the great powers who were seeking to take advantage of the disintegration of the Austro-Hungarian, Turkish, and Russian Empires. Balkanization was nothing other than the name that came to be attached to a disintegration unmitigated by a countervailing effort at a unity of difference. Each fragment became a unity resisting integration or combination. The hostility was not directed against the old regimes by an alliance of the dissatisfied but by each national grouping seeking out its own particular interests. The outcome was not cooperation and collaboration of ethnic and national diversities to attain common ends and goals frustrated by the old regimes but hostility toward each other as territorial claims of one nationality clashed with those of another.

Thus we see that, historically, a universal economic system, geared by an internal dynamic predisposing it to innovation, development, self-renovation, and global outreach, was encapsulated within territorial nation-states subversive of its driving principle. To preserve the economic prerogatives of its entrepreneurs, each nation-state framed discriminatory legislation. Instead of allowing capital, labor, and talent to respond with competitive efficiency, each nation sought competitive advantage by a variety of instrumentalities, such as tariffs. Instead of collaborating with each other to mount a decisive onslaught against precapitalism and its disintegrating structures in Central and Eastern Europe, they vied with each other in courting the dynastic heads of the old regimes. And most disastrous of all, instead of extending capitalism to the underdeveloped world, each nation-state enclave embarked on a policy of parasitic and predatory exploitation. Imperialism sacrificed the principle of global capitalistic development to the particularistic interests of national groupings of capitalists. For the latter, "Capitalism at home, precapitalism abroad" was the fundamental, even if unarticulated, slogan. The goal was to export not capitalism but linsey-woolsey; not to seed the capitalist revolution but to strangle it. Nation-state imperialism—the name that I give to that form of capitalism that developed its major sources of profit from the preservation of precapitalist societies and precapitalist labor systems—looked to the underdeveloped lands (1) as rich sources of primary products which could be most effectively exploited by cheap and abundant native labor, and (2) as markets for cheap manufactured goods, especially textiles. Nation-state imperialism was thus far more interested in protecting its cheap sources of labor than in laying down the expensive economic infrastructure for capitalistic development. Each of the great European imperial powers underpinned, rather than undermined, with its coercive power, the old ruling elites. The prospect of both widening markets and opportunities for the export of capital was not nearly as attractive as the perennial windfalls of a semiservile labor force in the colonies producing cheap food for European workers, cheap raw materials for European factories, and a high rate of return on capital invested in precapitalist systems. Just as the American planter-capitalist in the South anticipated a higher profit from slave than from free labor, so the nation-state imperialist capitalist reaped higher returns from coolie than from unionized labor. These windfalls proved to be both powerful deterrents to the spread of capitalism throughout the world and powerful provocations to destructive rivalries between the imperialist and would-be imperialist nation-states.

The entrapment of capitalism within nation-states had other deleterious consequences. No European state attained permanent hegemony over more than a fraction of the Continent. Even the largest nation-state enclosed a very limited internal market, a market quickly saturated by growing technological efficiency. The extension of the market beyond national borders was more and more inhibited as each capitalistic nation-state sought to protect its internal market from alien intrusion. Expansion was essential for capitalistic development; yet within the system of nation-states such expansion could be effected only by altering territorial boundaries by force. The alternative was imperialism, with its distortive effects on the allocation of capital and the manufactured product-mix; i.e. a flow of capital to precapitalist societies and a drying up of incentives for mass production, resulting in a widening internal market strikingly illustrated by the failure of the automobile industry in Europe to manufacture a cheap mass-produced car.

But the imperialist alternative was itself fraught with danger. The colonial holdings of the imperialist nation-states were frequently contiguous and provocative of rivalry; the adjudication of claims rested ultimately on coercive power; and new imperial aspirants were looked upon as interlopers. When, therefore, Germany emerged as the nation-state with the most advanced and efficient forms of capitalism and hence with the most imperious need to expand both territorially in Europe and imperialistically abroad, it found itself blocked by the existing nation-state system in Europe and its imperial extensions. There was, so it seemed, no alternative to war; for to remain passive was to invite catastrophic economic breakdown, while to embark on war offered a fighting chance that territorial borders in Europe might be rearranged and imperial holdings secured. To

166

break through the constraining limitations of the nation-state system, Germany joined up with precapitalistic, dynastic Austria-Hungary against precapitalist Tsarist Russia and her capitalist allies, France, England, and ultimately the United States. This was the grimmest paradox of all: capitalists and precapitalists in alliance rather than at war; and capitalist states at war with each other rather than with the systems blocking capitalistic development. Instead of the ringing slogan, "Capitalists of the world unite, for you have a world to build," the leaders of England, France, Germany, and the United States conjured up the frightening specter of barbaric hordes sweeping civilization away, as they stoked the fires of a patriotism so impassioned and so impervious to reason that the most noble and the most sensitive longed to kill or be killed.

The entrapment of the capitalistic global dynamic within the limits of the historically fortuitous nation-state system had other corrosive consequences. Nowhere in Europe did the capitalist revolution sweep the old order completely away. In every country, the revolutionary thrust was blunted by the power of the old regime to wrest compromises from the capitalist entrepreneurs in return for order and stability. Not only did precapitalist economic power continue to assert itself, but precapitalist political and ideational power did too. Whether it was England, France, or Germany, the monarchical and aristocratic principle retained, now more, now less, legitimacy. In even the most capitalistic nation-state of Europe, the officer class continued to be drawn from the old noble and aristocratic families. Established churches, now more, now less, still enjoyed at least symbolic primacy. Ideas

167

and values associated with the medieval world proved to be hardy perennials, strengthened through hybridization and cross-pollination with the new varieties seeded by the intellectual and scientific revolution. What men *thought* reality to be was far more motivational than what in *concrete fact* it was showing itself to be. The resiliency with which age-old symbolic forms adapted to the newly fashioned testifies strikingly to the autonomy of the mind as an active respondent to the press of external stimuli. These tenacious residuals were able to withstand the corrosive effects of capitalistic development because the nation-state rivalries placed a premium on emotional attachments to the fatherland. Patriotism was the great unifier because it could draw antagonistic classes into effective collaboration against external enemies threatening the existence of all. The capitalistic classes were thus caught up in a cul-de-sac from which there was no escape. On the one hand, the development of capitalism pressed for perennial reshaping of minds to the new economic realities; on the other hand, the danger inherent in nation-state rivalry called for the intensification of a patriotism that would not be pierced by rationality. This meant lending support to symbolic systems whose roots were in the precapitalist world. It meant encouraging the conforming to traditional religious motifs and to emotionally saturated symbols of loyalty to the state. It also meant tightening the alliances with the residuals of the old regime rather than loosening them. But above all it meant abandoning the revolutionary principle inherent within the capitalist dynamic.

The dilemma of the capitalist classes is mirrored in their reaction to the rise of the industrial proletariat. This proletariat was the handiwork of industrial capitalism, a form that had superseded the earlier mercantile one. The antagonism between worker and industrialist was an objective one, rooted in the drive of the capitalist for profit and the worker for subsistence. This objective tension lent itself to bitter and intense conflict, and to ideational exploitation. This tension was heightened by the prevailing assumption that industrial capitalism offered no secure promise of a rising standard of living for the working classes. The seedbed of Marxism was thus furrowed by a particular form of capitalism which did indeed press profits out of the hides of workers in mine and factory. Karl Marx translated this fact into an ideational system of seductive brilliance and impassioned righteousness. Recognizing that capitalism was an economic system that had bred revolutionary transformations, he assumed that it had exhausted its dynamic potential when it created the industrial proletariat. This was the end of the road for capitalistic development. Marx's theory of surplus value was meant to be the *coup de grâce*. Capitalism must be self-destructive because profits were dependent on the exploitation of the worker and there was bound to be a differential between what the worker produced and what he could buy back—a differential that doomed capitalism to ever-worsening crises and opened up for the proletariat recurring opportunities for supplanting capitalism with socialism. Marx assigned capitalism henceforth, in advanced countries, a reactionary role and delighted in exposing its cohabitation with the residuals of the old regimes. And among the sins of capitalism was its commitment to the nation-state. The global vision was now the dream of the proletariat. "Workers of the world unite"

169

was a slogan that comported well with the objective reality of the worker as a cog for machines everywhere the same—in England, France, Germany, and the United States. The worker had no fatherland, for his plight was universal. The worker in freeing himself would free the world.

Marx had a discerning eye and a mind of rare brilliance. He did indeed see what was there and he did indeed extrapolate from what he saw. But what he failed to do was to carry through his premises to their dialectical conclusions. If capitalism had already shown itself to be both developmental and revolutionary, if industrial capitalism was dialectically the outcome of capitalism's inner dynamic, what precluded the negation by capitalism itself of its own negation? What was there inherent in the capitalist dynamic that compelled it to settle for one of its temporal forms? Why might not industrial capitalism be simply a preparatory phase making ready the ground for a higher form of capitalism? Was it not possible that the very speeding up of the tempo of capital augmentation would create a pool of capital available for profitable investment in less-developed areas, such as the United States, that could mitigate the phase of primitive accumulation? Was this capital transfer not already occurring in Germany itself at the height of Marx's creativity? Was not the export of capital throughout Central and Eastern Europe and the Balkans already laying the groundwork for a spin-off into economic growth by picking up the initial tab for high infrastructure costs? Was it not also possible that raising the productivity of labor through the exploitation of capital might reduce the profitability of brawn and raise the profitability of brain with all the upgrading of the quality of the worker that such a substitution would necessitate? What a delightful dialectical tour de force! Capitalists driven by the profit motive to elevate man rather than degrade him. To free his mind and body rather than fetter and enslave them. To negate the negation: greed gives birth to altruism; selfishness to sharing; scarcity to abundance; constraints to freedom! Exploitation becomes profitless while human enrichment becomes the mother lode of capital accumulation!

Marx did not extrapolate such possibilities from the immanent dynamic of capitalism largely because the concrete capitalism of his day was brutal. Furthermore, the most advanced European capitalistic country of his day was England and not Germany. For Marx, England was the prototype. The anguish of primitive accumulation was the fate not of the pioneer and forerunner, but the inevitable destiny of all who followed. The emergence of industrial capitalism in England, however, was a historical fact, not a categorical imperative.

But what really blunted Marx's dialectical acumen was the evolution of capitalism *within* the nation-state system of Europe. Although he analyzed the capitalistic dynamic as though it were a universal, he did not follow through to the conclusion that the nation-state must be a more elemental and fundamental obstacle to capitalistic development than the industrial proletariat, for by blocking off expansion, the nation-state system doomed capitalistic development to ever-widening economic crises and depressions, with all the dangers to the capitalistic system that bitter, aggrieved, and hungry workers represent.

This hypothesis can be tested simply. The most destruc-

171

tive rivalries since 1860 in the advanced capitalistic countries have not been between capital and labor but between capital and capital: the American Civil War (industrial and free-farming capitalism vs. planter capitalism); the Franco-Prussian War (Prussian capitalism vs. French); World War I (English, French, and American capitalism vs. German capitalism). Is there any capital-labor struggle comparable? The suppression of the workers in the revolutions of 1848? The Paris Commune? The Pullman strike? What is also telling is the fact that in each of these major wars the worker proved to be more committed to his nation than to his class. Not only was he willing to lay down his life on the field of battle and to work long hours to produce the weapons for war, but he was ready to support moderate socialists in putting down by force his more radical fellow-workers. But most compelling is the evidence writ large in what Marxist leaders *did* in contrast with what they *said*. When the chips were down, the most distinguished Marxist scholars and the most respected Marxist politicians proclaimed that they had more in common with their national capitalist-class enemies than with alien working-class comrades. Workers of Germany unite, lest French workers overrun your land! Workers of France unite, lest the Huns sweep civilization away! The nation-state in 1914 had triumphed over capitalist and worker alike. The carnage at Verdun exposed both capitalists and workers as victims of the nation-state.

If then we retrospectively analyze the structural patterns that prevailed at the outbreak of World War I, we note that Europe was a system of nation-states, some predominantly capitalistic (England, France, Germany, Holland, Belgium, and Italy) and some predominantly precapitalist (Austria-Hungary, Turkey, and Russia). They were arrayed against each other, however, not along capitalist vs. precapitalist but along capitalist–precapitalist vs. capitalist–precapitalist lines. Each capitalist state aroused the fighting spirit of its people by an appeal to intense nationalism, and each precapitalist state by an appeal to dynastic patriotism. Each capitalist state was supported by its responsible Marxists on defensive grounds (the enemy state was the aggressor) and on developmental grounds (the enemy was a coalition of reactionary forces). Each noncapitalist state was a dynastic system riven by discontented national minorities and by aggrieved peasants and workers. England and France, for example, could call for the liberation of the suffering minorities and populations of the Austro-Hungarian and Turkish Empires, while Germany could champion the disgruntled of the Russian Empire. Each side could, and did, evoke fragmenting nationalist ideology to weaken its enemy.

The structural facts are thus highly revealing: World War I was not a capitalist alliance vs. a precapitalist alliance; it was not a combined effort of the developed countries to overthrow precapitalistic barriers to capitalistic expansion; it was not a storming of the barricades of the old regimes to proclaim the rights of man. Instead, World War I was a disastrous and murderous effort to advance or protect nation-state capitalism and imperialism, even if this meant aligning with and shoring up the decrepit and disintegrating precapitalist dynasties of Central and Eastern Europe and the Balkans. It was, in retrospect, a commitment to capitalistic entrapment within the nation-state rather than a commitment

173

to the global dynamic of capitalism and the overthrow of historically limiting barriers to its world-wide development.

The triumph of the nation-state over the universal principle left Europe a shambles, unleashed disintegrative trends within capitalism itself, tightened the determination to keep the underdeveloped peoples in thrall, and permitted the revolutionary principle to be usurped by a manipulative Marxist political elite. The story needs no retelling. Hemmed in by the limits of the nation-state, the developmental drive of capitalism was blunted and the system either stagnated (France, England, United States) or disintegrated (Italy, Germany). To the degree that stagnation threatened to deteriorate into chaotic collapse, totalitarian solutions (Fascism, Communism) became more and more appealing. Where capitalism did indeed collapse, as in Germany, the most responsible capitalist leaders saw no alternative to repressive totalitarianism and a renewed effort to break down the nation-state barriers to continental hegemony, a hegemony to be exercised through subjugation and enslavement and not through the extension of the partnership principle. The nation-state system had become so crippling that England and France preferred to appease Hitler rather than to defend by force the Versailles settlement. And when appeasement was abandoned, total war killed and maimed not only soldiers on the field of battle but millions of men, women, and children bombed into rubble and burned into ashes.

The nation-state system had once again revealed itself between World War I and World War II as antithetical to capitalistic development. It not only compelled the capitalist nationals of one nation-state to look upon their rivals in another nation-state as mortal enemies, but also opened wide Eastern Europe to an anticapitalist elite. The areas of European underdevelopment that would have widened opportunities for capitalistic development were cut off by the Bolshevik Revolution. The so-called *cordon sanitaire* was not a penetrative salient but a congerie of nonviable, dependent nation-states surviving as best they could by serving the great powers and by intoxicating themselves with the heady brew of nationalism.

The Soviet state not only blocked territorial expansion in Europe but helped to corrode nation-state capitalism in the West as well. It attributed the destructiveness of World War I to the capitalist system and not to its entrapment within the nation-state. It likewise attributed the stagnation and collapse of capitalism in the thirties to inner contradictions of capitalism and not to the blunting of its developmental principle. It stressed the inevitability of economic crises and depressions and the impoverishment of the working masses. It exposed imperialism as a vital concomitant of capitalism rather than as a malignancy. It denounced capitalism as the breeder of reaction and counterrevolution, and antithetical to the revolutionary principle. And when one looked at the shambles of postwar Europe, and when one experienced the Depression, and when one witnessed the wild growth of Fascism and the call by the leaders of the most powerful capitalist power of Europe, England, to appease rather than oppose, and when one glimpsed the degrading poverty and the agonized suffering of the underdeveloped peoples, it was not so easy to parry the Marxists or to counter the claims of the Soviet Union to be the bearer of salvation. Even if

175

one penetrated the Soviet façade and discovered its totalitarian character—that the Soviet system was no less totalitarian than Nazism; that whatever economic development had been achieved was through a form of callous, primitive accumulation that no capitalist society had ever equaled even in the worst days of early industrialism; that the modernization process in the Soviet Union had been kept free of the bourgeois freedoms of personal liberty, representative government, freedom of thought, communication, and artistic endeavor; that it had taken a devastating toll not only of illiterate peasants but of the Bolshevik elite itself—one was still likely to find the solution to the capitalist crisis in "pure" Marxism or "undistorted" Leninism rather than in removing the nation-state barriers to the resumption of the worldwide capitalist revolution.

The unconditional surrender of both Germany and Japan may have ended World War II, but it did not dissolve the basic sources of warfare. There was indeed a rearrangement of powers, but there was no dissolution of rivalrous nation-state interests. Such illusions quickly evaporated with the outbreak of the Cold War as allies became enemies and enemies became allies. And, if we look at the world today, there still seems to be precious little evidence that we are on the road to a global community committed to and sustained by the principle of the unity of diversity and the diversity of unity. But, as I stressed at the outset, I am concerned with the powerful forces at work beneath the surface of events that even now are shaping a liberating future and laying the foundations for the *Age of Humanity*.

What are these powerful forces? A new form of capitalism, and an enlightened economic and political elite, and coercive power of sufficient magnitude to translate ideal goal into concrete realization. If the patterns of action are translated into the policies framed by the decision-makers, they reveal that the United States since World War II has dedicated itself to the revolutionary dynamic of developmental capitalism and has been carrying through the structuring of a global community rooted in integrative rather than nation-state sovereignty, and in inalienable natural rights rather than national, racial, or class rights.

To substantiate this hypothesis, I shall point out what the United States has *done* rather than what it has *said*, and draw the necessary implications from these acts.

1. The Marshall Plan, the Treaty of Rome, and the successful launching of the Common Market. These acts reveal a commitment to (a) economic growth and development, and (b) the undercutting of nation-state sovereignty by building a common economic foundation binding the nations together by common interests and by a joint sharing of the economic resources for war-making (the iron and coal community).

2. The rehabilitation and reconstruction of West Germany and Japan. These acts illustrate an awareness that causes of war reside in (a) effective coercive sovereignty, and (b) economic breakdown. Wars are not generated by national or racial or ideational presuppositions but by entrapment. To offset the former, both Germany and Japan signed treaties giving up claims to nuclear weapons, and to forestall the latter, they were launched on what has proved to be phenomenal economic growth and development.

3. An open-ended approach to the Soviet Union since the summit meeting in 1955, as revealed by the following actions:

(a) Private meetings between the heads of state at Camp David, Vienna, and Glassboro.

(b) Nuclear agreements: (1) Antarctica, (2) limited test ban, (3) nonproliferation, (4) establishment of the Hot Line, (5) ongoing SALT talks.

(c) Economic assistance: (1) periodic relaxation of categories of strategic goods that may be exported to the Soviet Union, (2) shipment of wheat to the Soviet Union, (3) economic aid to satellite states.

(d) Joint action, as in the Pakistan-India dispute over Kashmir.

These acts demonstrate that United States decision-makers may utilize ideology but they are not victimized by it. Flexible pragmatism and instrumentalism are reflected in the actions of every President and Secretary of State since World War II.

4. Support, both overt and covert, for the decolonization process in Africa, Asia, and the Middle East, along with a commitment to developmentalism everywhere. The anti-imperialist role of the United States has been, and still is, blurred by the fact that it had to operate simultaneously on two levels: (a) sustain alliances with states such as Holland, Belgium, France, and England with vital stakes in retaining imperial controls, and (b) support national movements seeking independence. To attain these seemingly contradictory goals, the United States gave covert support to national-

liberation movements while they were seeking independence, followed by formal recognition after they had achieved it.

The anti-imperialist policies of the United States are grounded in (1) the need to break down imperial barriers to the expansion of American capitalism; (2) the need for markets for sophisticated products, hence the necessity of raising the standard of living in underdeveloped lands; (3) the need to upgrade the quality of the labor supply to foster industrialization; and (4) the need to widen opportunities for capital investment by encouraging diversification. Structurally, American capitalism is driven to spread capitalism globally. Its highest profits are generated from capital-intensive investment rather than from labor-intensive. It needs a *brain* supply more than a *brawn* supply. Cheap primary commodities are not nearly as profitable as machine-made end-products. To effect this transformation, the United States must break up the traditional, precapitalist societies and restructure them so as to spin off growth and development. Imperialism, which was a source of profits for the nation-state capitalism of the late nineteenth and early twentieth century, is a deterrent to profits for a capital-intensive, brain-oriented global capitalism of the 1970's.

I grant that this anti-imperialist imperative is blurred by the rhetoric that has enveloped United States involvement in Southeast Asia and by the prevailing assumption that since capitalism went hand in hand with imperialism and underdevelopment, the one necessitates the other. As for the involvement in Southeast Asia, I can only point out that the privately owned capitalist press and the privately owned TV

179

media, as well as any number of prominent capitalist politicians, are overwhelmingly committed to withdrawal from Southeast Asia, to the turning over of the area to coalition governments sympathetic to the Viet Cong and Hanoi. I would also call your attention to the fact that President Nixon, not unsympathetic to capitalism, has publicly committed himself to withdrawal from Southeast Asia. I would therefore suggest that we suspend judgment as to what Vietnam was all about until, let us say, 1972, after England has withdrawn from Southeast Asia and after we are in a position to see whether or not American capitalism is indeed imperialistic.

I suggest withholding judgment on Vietnam because what is still inconclusive there is offset by what is manifestly evident elsewhere. The United States did not turn Japan into a colony, even though she had more than ample power and opportunity to do so. Japan was released for economic growth. The same holds true for Europe. The United States did not take advantage of Europe's weakness but encouraged and supported the building of a prosperous European community. In each instance, the United States preferred the building up of strong economies, even though this meant, on some levels, the build-up of powerful economic competition. The concept of a global capitalist system took precedence over the concept of nation-state rivalry.

And finally, United States support of Israel underlines the developmental commitments of global capitalism. Israel is to the Middle East what Japan is to Asia.

If the record is so clear with respect to both Japan and

Europe, can one really be sure that the United States is not equally committed to developmentalism throughout Asia, Africa, and South America? Does imperialism hold out for American capitalism profits at all commensurable with developmentalism?

5. A recommitment to the realization of the universals, those inalienable rights let loose by the first capitalist revolutions. These universals were formulated so as to create a climate conducive to the development of a free risk-taking individual. It is summed up in the notion that all men are created equal and are endowed with certain inalienable rights, among which are life, liberty, and the pursuit of happiness. The right of the individual to pursue happiness is dependent on the removal of man-made impediments to that pursuit.

Capitalistic development in the past only approximated these ideal goals. They remained unrealized because of (1) precapitalist vestiges, (2) nation-state entrapment, (3) intracapitalist rivalry, (4) the scarcity of capital, (5) the operation of the business cycle. All these factors made for waste and exploitation of human resources, for much suffering, for callous disregard of humane values.

Since World War II, but especially during the sixties, these deterrents were mitigated. Of special significance was the heightened awareness of how the capitalist system operates, along with the first clear-cut signs that compound interest is beginning to release its remarkable effects. A 4 percent growth rate compounded spells out undreamed-of wealth by the end of the century. This compounding opens

181

up for the first time the realistic possibility for the elimination of poverty, underprivilege, and the waste of human resources.

The remarkable augmentation of capital since World War II, the steady shift from labor-intensive to capital-intensive sources of profit, the spread of functional obsolescence, i.e., the creation of new technological processes enhancing the productivity of labor and the expansion of markets—the gestation of a world economy—all these factors are spinning off the discontents and the revolutions of our time. (The black revolution, the student revolution, the anti-imperialist revolution—these are nothing other than capitalistically spawned.) Developing capitalism is on the march once again and it is undercutting, eroding, and overthrowing precapitalist systems and obsolescing forms and values of nation-state imperialism. The pain, the agony, the suffering, the disruption we are now undergoing are but the outward manifestations of the collapse of nation-state imperialism with its destructive rivalries, callous exploitation, and hypocritical value system, and the laying of the foundations for a global community whose ever-growing wealth—compounded daily—will release man from the grip of scarcity and spin him off into the realms of spiritual freedom. Securely supported by the quantification of material goods, he will be free to enrich the quality of his living.

I have deliberately held off till now any discussion of what this analysis means for Jews and Judaism. And with good reason. It permits me to formulate several simple generalizations that can now be tested in the light of my overall thesis. The history of the Jews and of Judaism since the sixteenth century is vitally related to the vicissitudes of capitalistic development. If one charts the lines of capitalistic development, one is simultaneously charting the crucial lines of Jewish history in the Western world. This, I suggest, is what one will discover:

(1) To the degree that developing capitalism (till 1914) penetrated a territorial sector and restructured it, to that degree did Jews attain freedom of settlement and freedom from medieval and traditional restraints and discrimination (Holland, England, United States, France, Germany).

(2) To the degree that developing capitalism failed to penetrate and restructure, to that degree did Jews continue to suffer from restraints and discrimination (Eastern Europe).

(3) To the degree that capitalism underwent crises, stagnation, and disintegration, to that degree did Jews prove to be vulnerable and, in extreme instances (Nazi Germany), dispensable.

(4) To the degree that a Marxist elite took over the Westernization and modernization process, to that degree did Jews find their status in jeopardy (U.S.S.R.).

(5) To the degree that capitalism has revived in the West since World War II, to that degree have the vestigial restrictions on Jewish freedom been eliminated and nonrational barriers to integration dismantled.

(6) To the degree that developing capitalism penetrated and restructured any area, to that degree did it free Jews from traditional religious and ideational restraints and open up for them a wide spectrum of spiritual and ideational op-

183

tions (Reform, Conservative, and Westernized–Orthodox Judaisms; Haskalah, secularist, and nationalist ideologies).

These generalizations can be simply tested by the experience of the Jews in the United States, Germany, and Russia. By any measure, the United States represents the society where developmental capitalism has been most successful. It is also the society in which Jews have enjoyed the most freedom and the widest range of economic, political, social, cultural, and religious opportunity.

The Jews of Germany were emancipated in the latter part of the nineteenth century by the development of capitalism, but this emancipation was tainted by the failure of the capitalist revolution to dismantle thoroughly the foundations of the old regimes. When, following the economic collapse of 1929, German capitalism disintegrated and capitalists in desperation threw their support to Nazism, the Jews were stripped of their rights, deprived of their wealth, and assigned to extermination.

In Tsarist Russia, capitalism had made insufficient headway by 1914 to underpin a successful revolution against the old regime, with the result that the Jews continued to suffer discrimination and persecution. When the revolution did break out, it was taken over by the Bolsheviks, who established an anticapitalist regime committed to modernization and Westernization. From the very outset, the position of the Jews was precarious because of their nonproletarian, nonpeasant class status. Most recently, the Jews have been subjected to a kind of discriminatory treatment that threatens their survival. The disintegration of Jewry in the Soviet Union is to be attributed to the failure of the Bolshevik sys-

tem to sustain economic growth without profit-seeking entrepreneurs. The failure to solve the problem of productivity
in agriculture continuously exposes the Russian population
to a restricted food supply and renders them highly suscept-
ible to diversionary anti-Semitism. Such susceptibility is ag-
gravated by the chronic housing shortage and the scarcity
and shoddy quality of consumer goods.

The upshot of this analysis leads to simple conclusions.
Developmental capitalism is the only economic system that
has proved its capacity for wealth augmentation; it is also
the only economic system that has generated noneconomic
ideational concomitants upholding the freedom of the individual to explore reality without traditional constraints. No
operative Marxist society has been able to sustain economic
growth, to spur agricultural production—i.e., feed its people, without recourse to capitalist nations—to underwrite
individual freedom, or to tolerate the free exploration of
reality by sensitive minds or spirits. Indeed, the only free
market for Marxism, where all existing and novel varieties of
Marxist thought can be freely disseminated, is in the capitalist world. The *concrete* record would seem to underwrite
the following prognosis: to the degree that global capitalism
carries through a successful revolution against precapitalism
and nation-state imperialism, to that degree does it promise to
create economic abundance and to release the universals securing individual freedom. Contrariwise, to the degree that
it fails, to that degree does it open up the dreaded possibilities of totalitarianism of both left and right. And to the degree that Marxist elites seek to modernize and Westernize
without the utilization of the profit motive, to that degree

do they doom their societies to both starvation *and* unfreedom. Let me stress this last point once again. Without Western wheat, the Soviet Union would in the past few years have faced the prospect of famine; without Western wheat, Communist China *right now* would face famine. To paraphrase a comment by the former Secretary of Agriculture Orville Freeman: if the Marxists took over the world, who would feed them?

It is because I am convinced that we are witnessing the rebirth of the capitalist revolution that the tumults of the time do not drive me to despair. The old regimes are toppling once again because global capitalism is breaking down the nation-state imperialist barriers to economic growth and is furrowing the soil for a new burst of freedom for man. It is even now, beneath the grim surface of events, laying the foundations for the *Age of Humanity*.

To the building of these foundations, I would hope that Temple Emanu-El, under its enlightened rabbinical and lay leadership, would lend its hand. It was the revolutionary thrust of developmental capitalism in the United States that nurtured the birth of the Reform movement in this country. Among the inalienable rights that it vouchsafed was the right of the individual to have the religion of his choice and the right of the religious spirit to search unafraid for as yet unknown attributes of God. Temple Emanu-El was one of the first fruits of the radical religious spirit. It affirmed that Judaism was not simply a religion of the past, or only a religion of the present, but a religion for the future as well. Its rabbis and leaders committed themselves to the task of spiritualizing the Westernization and the modernization process rather than obstructing or deterring it. They had faith that God had instilled within man a longing for perfection through freedom and for freedom. The godly man, for them, was one who walked erect because he preferred the risks of error to the security of traditional truths.

I am confident that when yesterday becomes tomorrow, it will reveal that Temple Emanu-El was loyal to the principles on which it was founded: that at a time when the pangs of birth were mistaken for the agony of death, its rabbis and leaders discerned the distinction.

125th Anniversary Worship Service
April 11, 1970

A Reform of Reform

DANIEL JEREMY SILVER
Rabbi, The Temple, Cleveland, Ohio

It is a privilege and pleasure for me to be here as part of this 125th anniversary celebration of Temple Emanu-El. I confess, however, that I am not quite certain what my role should be. Certainly you did not invite me to rehearse Emanu-El's chronicle of achievement. These are your achievements. You wrote this history. You have for long been the largest congregation in the largest Jewish community in the world. Your buildings have been landmarks in this city. Your leadership and your membership have been active in all that has made for the progress and prosperity of New York.

Perhaps the success of Emanu-El suggests something of what I ought to say. There are always those who feel that simply by affiliating with a premier congregation they are among the faithful and have assured themselves of a first-rate faith. Faith cannot be had simply by enrolling oneself in a temple register. Faith cannot be had by delegating the responsibilities and activities of religious life to an institution, however significant that institution may be. Faith must be won, it must be searched for, it must be wrestled with. Faith is an active undertaking.

Before coming, I went back and read a bit of the history of Emanu-El and discovered that some fifty years ago at a celebration much like this one Rabbi Enelow chose to speak these words:

> The most serious problem today lies in vicarious Judaism. All too large is the number of those who are content with passive membership in the community and in its organizations. The actual conduct of religious life they leave to others, but no religious life can flourish by delegation. The Jew has never believed in vicariousness in matters of faith.

In his day and in ours there are Jews who practice vicariousness in matters of faith. "I belong. I pay my assessments. My children go to the religious school. My daughter's marriage was solemnized by the rabbi. I attend occasionally on the High Holy Days—that's it, isn't it?" Of course, that's precisely not it!

Whatever else our age is or is not, it is a convulsed age—an age of confusing change. Our times force us to ask ourselves again and again: What is demanded of me and by whom? Old assumptions are no longer taken for granted. Is there a new morality? What are the new moralities? What is the way that I should go? What are the standards by which I should abide? How can I achieve significantly? How can I find peace of mind and happiness? Never has an age had so much: so much opportunity, so much freedom, so many nervous breakdowns, so many young people walking around with dead, sullen faces. We are confused, we need desperately the balanced theological understandings of Jewish thought and the high moral reach of Jewish ethic. For many, Judaism and life pass each other by because they have confused the institution with that which takes place within the institution, the envelope with the substance of the letter. He wore an open shirt, he had beads around his neck, he was unshod, he spoke with a smile, and in a deliberately soft voice he said to me, "You know, I'm not the one who dropped out, but my parents have. They live for things. They live to see and to be seen. They say what everybody else is saying. They read what everybody else is reading. They go to synagogue when everybody else gets dressed up. It is not that they don't know, it is that they no longer care to ask the questions."

Never in Scripture is it said: "Join a congregation and gain faith." Again and again it is said: *Darshu-ni Veyihyu*, "Seek ye Me, and live." Faith begins in personal search. We are called the Children of Israel. Why? Israel is Jacob's second name, the name Jacob earned after he had wrestled the long night with the angel, with his conscience, with the sunshine and the shadows, with his love and his fears, with his hopes and his tribulations, and had not been overcome. Faith is to expose oneself to life, to all the uncertainties, to all the

190

incongruities, to all the confusion, to the madding throng, to others, and not quail; faith is to dare to live, to be receptive to life. If we are truly sons of Emanu-El, Emanu-El —God is with us—then we have to be willing to let God in, and we will not find God simply by occasionally walking in these doors. We must walk in these doors with a certain receptivity. We must be willing to bare the quick flesh of our souls, to be hurt by life, to care for another human being, to dare for a cause; if need be, to change the pattern of our lives. Only as we touch others can we touch God. Where is God? God, as the Hassid said, is wherever man lets Him in.

So far I have offered an appropriate, typical anniversary sermon; thoughts which ought to be said and are often said on such occasions as this, but I submit that such thoughts are only part of the proper and necessary meaning of this morning.

Another question must be faced. Simply put, it is this: What happens when someone walks in these doors and says, "I am willing, I do care, I want to understand. I need to know. Help me"? How supportive, how enlightening, how responsive, how effective are our religious institutions?

I am afraid that when we look at our institutions, if we use an anniversary to look back and look ahead, we will be forced to admit that much of what we do in this congregation, in any congregation, must be categorized under such titles as the spinning of wheels or familiar but purely formal routine—what we do simply because it always has been done, words which have been spoken because they were once appropriate, not necessarily because they touch another soul.

When I wondered how I might develop this point for you, I reminded myself that I had in my library a book, a prayerbook, your prayerbook, an *Order of Prayer for Divine Service* written by and for this congregation by your first rabbi, Leo Merzbacher. I need hardly remind you that Emanu-El came into being out of "Cultus Verein," a small group of men who banded together "to create such a service that shall arouse and quicken devotion and thus uplift the heart of God." They wanted a living, vibrant faith. They wanted Judaism to speak to them effectively, in the language of their day. Out of that need came this book of worship. It is a fine, beautiful book. It is good to hold. More than this, it offers what was certainly for its day an effective and harmonious service, and one which was among the significant creations in early Reform liturgy.

But what has this book to do with the question of priority and purpose in congregational life? Simply this. Rabbi Merzbacher had the good sense to preface his order, his liturgy, with an explanation of the text. Why he had made certain selections. Why certain paragraphs had been excised. Why the prayers were arranged as they were arranged. I often wish our *Union Prayerbook* contained such an explanation which we might mull over in the quiet of the preworship moments. In any case, after addressing a few words to those who would pick up this book when they came to worship, he addressed a few words to the religious establishment of his day, those whom he felt would pick up this book and be put off and displeased by the changes which he had suggested:

Lay aside this Prayerbook, with a smile, if you please, or with scorn, if you choose . . . be only kind enough to give us some credit for sincerity, how different soever our ideas may be from yours, and our ways from your ways, and be reminded of the saying of our sages: *Kol Mahloket she-hi Leshem Shamayim So Fah lehitkayem.* "Every discord for a holy purpose, tends in the end to a consolidation."

In any event, the reforms of his service became familiar. The Jewish community adjusted to liturgical variety and, with acceptance, the religious rebels of yesterday became the religious Establishment of our day. I wonder if we accord our critics the same credit for sincerity which Rabbi Merzbacher pleaded for a hundred and more years ago; for there is criticism, all is not right in the household of religion. The votes are being taken, people are voting with their feet and by their votes they are saying: What you do is not so much in error as irrelevant. We do not take exception to your activities but there's no bite in them, they do not touch us, Judaism is bland, it is not alive. The young do not even bother to demonstrate against us. I suspect that what we must do on an anniversary is to ask ourselves again some fundamental questions. Why does a synagogue exist? Why does my congregation exist? And then ask ourselves: How well do our programs and activities achieve these ends?

Why does a congregation exist? I would suggest that a congregation exists for a single purpose, and that is to encourage the man, the woman, the young person to seek the ultimate religious achievement—*Kedusha*—holiness, and to guide and support him on that way. Holiness is the supreme

193

religious virtue: *Kedoshim Ti-hyu Ki Kadosh Ani Adonai Elohehem,* "Holy thou shalt be for I, the Lord, your God, am holy." And what is holiness? We Jews have always had a particular and special definition of holiness. Holiness is not ritual exuberance. Holiness is not fasting, midnight vigils, endless lacerations, bloody flagellations, exhibitionist piety. Holiness is a particular way of life, moral self-discipline, devotion in act to that wisdom which separates the trivial and the tinsel from the significant, a way of life which is sanctified and concerned, sensitive to human values, in which every human being is sacred.

Throughout the community of Israel these weeks, we are reading from the Book of Leviticus. The Book of Leviticus is essentially one long definition of *Kedusha,* holiness. How is one to become holy? By not bearing a grudge, by taking up a stumbling block from before the blind, by dealing openly and honestly with one's neighbor, by honoring one's parents, by fearing God. That is the way of holiness, and that is the way a congregation exists to encourage. Why do we have worship—daily worship, weekly worship? So that we may breathe an hour a day, a few hours a week, the atmosphere of *Kedusha,* good clean spiritual air, so that we may enter again and again a symbolic environment which will underscore the gap between holiness and the ordinary, the vulgar, and the humdrum. Why do we have learning in a congregation? So that we can take the basic ageless disciplines and relate them effectively to the complex decisions of our lives. And why is there congregation? Because we cannot do it alone, because we need help, because we need to meet, to touch, and to learn how to cooperate with each

194

other. That is what a congregation is all about. Are we effectively promoting *Kedusha* or do we turn off the young and the middle-aged and the older who come searching? Do we present the shadow or the substance, platitudes or the living word, empty forms or meaningful participant ritual, theoretical talk or the experience of belonging to an historic people?

Reform Judaism, dear friends, came into being in order to make our faith vital, significant. Those who cared nothing about Judaism walked away. Those who cared deeply for Judaism sought to renew it. They took a Judaism that had become lush and ritually overgrown during the enforced parochial experience of the Middle Ages and tried to cut away the underbrush so that one could walk freely about and see clearly the outline of the tall majestic trees— the central affirmations. Our faith had become community bound. We needed to learn to live with others. Judaism was tied to premodern aesthetics and attitudes. We needed to draw on new standards of beauty and from the teaching and the wisdom of the new sciences. We sought to create a way of life which would be understandable to the citizen of the nineteenth century, and since that age was optimistic, confident of man, individualistic, reformist, respectable, our congregations were molded in that image.

I would suggest that we have come to that point in our history where we need a reform of Reform, for what we did then is now no longer that vital. That Reform spoke to a particular need which is no longer our need, to a particular Jew who is no longer our congregant. That age was bourgeois—good and solid, full of good and solid middle-class virtues. It was respectable and community-minded. It knew not Auschwitz, Hiroshima, or Watts. We live in darker days, our lives are far more shadowed, our needs are far more urgent. Our world is convulsed. We have lost confidence in progress. Optimism has been drained from us. We wonder whether civilization, man, can survive. People want something more than sweet reasonableness from the pulpit. They want something more than simple dignity from worship. They need to touch other lives, not to worship next to strangers. They want to feel, they want a living faith, a faith that encourages, engages life, ennobles.

All over our country there are tens of hundreds of young Jews who are taking courses in Oriental mysticism. Why? Because familiar worship patterns, our worship, do not satisfy their spiritual needs. They want something more intense, something in which they can be more involved, in which there is more movement, more highlight, more depth. All around our country there are hundreds of young and middle-aged Jews who suffer for every injustice save those done to their people; why? Because Judaism has been to them a matter of words on a Saturday morning, not a life-style or a mission. All around our country there are many among the middle-aged and elderly who rarely walk into the synagogue because they find that it no longer is as meaningful as it once was. Words are spoken, familiar words. Rites are celebrated, familiar rites. But they have changed and somehow the synagogue has not changed with them. We speak in terms and in forms beloved and familiar a generation ago, but we do not speak with the idiom of the contemporary or with the forms of today.

Dear friends, the *Union Prayerbook* was not given to Moses on Mt. Sinai. There is no rule that worship must be carried out ever and always with a grand cathedral organ and a robed choir in the way in which it was orchestrated these past decades. Aaron did not submit to the tribes of Israel a religious school curriculum which had to be held fast to from then and forever. Miriam was never president of a sisterhood. What we did was good and valid a generation ago. I am suggesting that now we must do other things in other ways; find more effective ways to transmit the ancient insights, the teaching and the understanding. These insights have not been outmoded. Never have they been more needed. It is simply that we are different. We speak a different language, we dance to different tunes, we sing different melodies. Can we truly say that our synagogues sing our melodies, speak our language, dance to our tune, answer our questions, sometimes? always?

All over our land, one thing is clear. There is a desperate search. We are part of it. We are frustrated, bitter. We are confused. What must I do? How shall I live? What are the proper and functional standards of family life? What represents truth? How do I go about effecting social change? How do I go about changing myself? How do I learn to live with other human beings, to touch them, not simply use them; to be part of a community, not partner to a society which manipulates and abuses people?

The synagogue, this synagogue, has much to teach and has men who can teach. What is needed is a willingness to break out of the old modes, break the *kelipah*, the hardened shell, to go about our business untrammeled by the conven-

197

tions of the past, so that the voice of the past can again be heard.

What I am saying to you is not simply another pop-culture plea to be "with it." Let me quote to you from one of your own rabbis, Samuel Goldenson, from a speech he made thirty-five years ago:

Our energies, therefore, should be engaged in strengthening and reinforcing every wall and every pillar of our religious structure. . . . We must bring the sustaining and life-giving nourishment to them directly, with such zeal and enthusiasm, with such force and consecration, that they will be drawn to us.

In a word, the problem is for us to reassert and reaffirm spiritual content, not by word of mouth merely but by example, an example that shall emanate from genuine feeling and a heartfelt appreciation of their pertinence and sublimity.

As there are some who are leaving the synagogue because we failed to stress the personal and the mystic sides of our faith, so there are others who have become indifferent to the religion of their fathers because their grievances and resentments against a world in which brute inequality and selfish materialism reign are not sufficiently voiced. We can draw them back only by assuming once more the role of the prophets in Israel and preach the simple and unmistakable yet elemental doctrine, "Not by might nor by power does man prevail but by the spirit of God." Our message, therefore, should be social and communal, as well as personal and mystic, to the end that "righteousness shall flow as water and justice as a mighty stream."

I have suggested that over the years our congregations have become one-dimensional. We have spoken with mild tones to the middle-aged about middle-class values. We must become multidimensional; speak to the street urchin, to the rebellious youngster, to the confused young person, to those beginning a family and worrying through the problems of love, to the middle-aged and the aging, each in his own language, each in terms appropriate to their needs and to their understanding. We have the teaching, we have the wisdom, we have the resources. What we lack are appropriate forms and idioms, and we suffer from being hidebound. You have to help us in finding the ways. You have to encourage us to break out of the familiar routines into new avenues of religious undertaking. You have to encourage us by coming, by searching, by seeking, because no institution can remake your faith and give you new strength unless you are willing to come, to be part of its life, of its worship, of its liturgy, of its learning. You have a proud and noble record, a history second to none. You understand the imperatives of learning and of love of God, of Israel, and of mankind. You have the resources of person and profession. You stand on the threshold of a potentially great era of service. Walk into it with fresh eyes, clear minds, burdened by concern but not by the past.

May the Lord establish the work of your hands, yea the work of your hands may He establish it.

AMEN

199

Office of the Mayor

CITY OF NEW YORK

Proclamation

Whereas: THE YEAR 1970 MARKS THE 125TH ANNIVERSARY OF THE FOUNDING, AT GRAND AND CLINTON STREETS IN LOWER MANHATTAN, OF CONGREGATION EMANU-EL OF THE CITY OF NEW YORK, AND

WHEREAS: FROM ITS INCEPTION THE CONGREGATION HAS BEEN A VITAL FORCE IN THE LIFE AND SPIRITUAL GROWTH OF THIS CITY, AND

WHEREAS: ITS MEMBERS HAVE TRADITIONALLY PROVIDED THE CITY, STATE, NATION AND FREE WORLD WITH A HOST OF DISTINGUISHED PUBLIC SERVANTS AND WITH LEADERS IN THE FIELDS OF MEDICINE, LAW, EDUCATION, COMMERCE AND THE ARTS, AND

WHEREAS: THE PHYSICAL PRESENCE, AT 65TH STREET AND FIFTH AVENUE, OF THIS HALLOWED INSTITUTION, LARGEST JEWISH HOUSE OF WORSHIP IN THE WORLD, A DESIGNATED LANDMARK AND SHRINE FOR VISITORS FROM ALL OVER THE WORLD, HAS CONTINUALLY SERVED THE ENTIRE COMMUNITY, REGARDLESS OF RACE, COLOR OR CREED -- AS EXEMPLIFIED BY THE HOSPITALITY ENJOYED BY 1,350,000 ALLIED SERVICEMEN DURING WORLD WAR II, AND

WHEREAS: THE PRESENT RABBIS, OFFICERS AND TRUSTEES OF THIS VENERABLE CONGREGATION DEVOTE SO MUCH OF THEIR TIME AND ENERGIES TO THE BETTERMENT OF CONTEMPORARY NEW YORK IN THE FINEST TRADITION OF THEIR PREDECESSORS,

NOW, THEREFORE, I, JOHN V. LINDSAY, MAYOR OF THE CITY OF NEW YORK, DO HEREBY PROCLAIM APRIL 11, 1970, AS

"TEMPLE EMANU-EL DAY"

IN NEW YORK CITY, AS AN EXPRESSION OF APPRECIATION OF THE PEOPLE OF THIS CITY FOR THE CONTRIBUTIONS OF CONGREGATION EMANU-EL OF THE CITY OF NEW YORK TO THE SPIRITUAL, CULTURAL AND MATERIAL WELFARE OF ALL OUR PEOPLE.

IN WITNESS WHEREOF I HAVE HEREUNTO SET MY HAND AND CAUSED THE SEAL OF THE CITY OF NEW YORK TO BE AFFIXED.

John V. Lindsay
MAYOR, THE CITY OF NEW YORK

RABBIS OF THE CONGREGATION

Leo Merzbacher
Samuel Adler
James K. Gutheim
Gustav Gottheil
Joseph Silverman
Judah Leon Magnes
Hyman G. Enelow
Nathan Krass
Samuel Schulman
Samuel H. Goldenson
Julius Mark
Nathan A. Perilman

Associate
Ronald B. Sobel

Assistant
Mark N. Goldman

PRESIDENTS OF THE CONGREGATION

Isaac Dittenhoefer
Abraham Michelbacher
Lewis May
James Seligman
Louis Marshall
Irving Lehman
Lewis L. Strauss
Saul F. Dribben
Alfred R. Bachrach
Alvin E. Coleman

125TH ANNIVERSARY LECTURE SERIES

November 9, 1969	Earl Ubell
November 16, 1969	Milton Himmelfarb
November 23, 1969	Bayard Rustin
November 30, 1969	Marshall Sklare
December 7, 1969	Krister Stendahl
March 1, 1970	Morris B. Abram
March 8, 1970	Abraham Kaplan
March 15, 1970	Edward Flannery
March 22, 1970	Eugene Borowitz
March 29, 1970	Ellis Rivkin

MUSICAL EVENTS

Organ Recitals

April 5, 1970	John Huston
April 12, 1970	Searle Wright
April 19, 1970	Frederick Swann
April 26, 1970	John Haney

Festival Concert

Concluding the Anniversary Celebration, on Sunday, May 3, 1970, the Emanu-El Choir, under the direction of Richard Korn, presented a program of music composed under the sponsorship of the Congregation.

Sabbath Services in the Temple
at 10:30 a.m.

Anniversary Guest Preacher

Rev. Dr. Daniel Jeremy Silver

The Temple, Cleveland, Ohio

———◆———

Anniversary Luncheon

GRAND BALLROOM, THE PIERRE, 12:30 P.M.

Introduction ....Mr. Herbert C. Bernard
National Anthem ....Cantor Arthur Wolfson
Invocation ....Rabbi Ronald B. Sobel
Welcome ....Mr. Alvin E. Coleman

Greetings
Remarks ....Rev. Dr. Julius Mark
Rev. Dr. Nathan A. Perilman
Benediction ....Rabbi Mark N. Goldman

204

ANNIVERSARY PLANNING COMMITTEE

Herbert C. Bernard . . . .*Chairman*

Alfred R. Bachrach	Walter S. Mack
Robert W. Bloch	Rev. Dr. Julius Mark
Mrs. Ingram S. Carner	John B. Oakes
Alvin E. Coleman	Morton Pepper
Mrs. Chester S. Friedman	Rev. Dr. Nathan A. Perilman
Henry Fruhauf	Mervin H. Riseman
Rabbi Mark N. Goldman	Daniel S. W. Schrank
Mrs. Robert E. Herman	Rabbi Ronald B. Sobel
Mrs. Alan Kirschberg	Admiral Lewis L. Strauss
Samuel Kleiman	Lester J. Waldman
Richard K. Korn	Cantor Arthur Wolfson

ASSISTED BY THE "COMMITTEE OF 125"